PRAISE FOR *NAMING THE UNNAMEABLE*

"What a magnificent symphony of sacred names! My heart is resounding with the music Matthew Fox has evoked in this celebration of the manifold attributes of a Being he gleefully admits transcends all naming. By weaving in the voices of philosophers, theologians and mystics across the spiritual tradition, Fox grounds this magnificent offering even more deeply, inviting us to participate in a space of ongoing inquiry."

—MIRABAI STARR, author of *Caravan of No Despair*

"I've always experienced the Divine as expressing through everything around me: the squirrel chattering up the oak tree, the waves crashing on the shore, my baby boy looking me in the eyes. Matthew Fox in *Naming the Unnameable* allows us to explore all of the many and dynamic ways that God speaks and breathes and plays in the world."

—JENNIFER BERIT LISTUG, co-author with Matthew Fox and Skylar Wilson of *Order of the Sacred Earth*

"This is a simple book written by a brilliant man who gives us a democratic vision of the names of God. It will be sure to appeal to readers of many faiths, scientists, and nature lovers as well."

—STEVEN HERRMAN

T0098896

"These are not just names but 89 theories of God across the ages and the planet, each focusing on the characteristic it deems most divine. Matthew Fox leads us on a startling and beautiful journey through humanity's capacity to envision God, showing every way of looking at God is legitimate if it raises the aspirations of its adherents and their ability to carry them out. Is there objectively a God? What 'God' even means explodes in this little book like fireworks in the mind."

—Nancy Abrams, author of *A God That Could Be Real*

"Matthew Fox leads us on an important yet easily absorbable exploration of the multiplicity of forms in which we perceive the Divine in our lives. While we so readily seek to differentiate, define or even dispel the sacred, we desperately need teachers like Fox who show us the unity in diversity. I suspect that anyone can find some names in this book that resonate for them, whether scientist or artist, believer or atheist, old or young, female or male. Fox's depth of insight and abundant compassion is felt throughout the pages as he helps us embrace and share in the wholeness of who We are."

—SKY NELSON-ISAACS, M.Sc. Physics
and author of *Living in Flow*

Naming the Unnameable

89 Wonderful and Useful Names for God...
Including the Unnameable God

Naming the Unnameable

89 Wonderful and Useful Names for God
...Including the Unnameable God

MATTHEW FOX

LITTLE BOUND BOOKS
Small Books, Big Impact

LITTLE BOUND BOOKS
Small Books. Big Impact | *www.littleboundbooks.com*

First Edition Paperback
ISBN 978-1-947003-94-1

Published by Little Bound Books, *an imprint of Homebound Publications*
Front Cover Image © The Black Madonna
by Ullrrich Javier Lemus | Visit www.ullrrich.com
Cover and Interior Designed by Leslie M. Browning

Permission is granted by:
 Jonathan Star for citations from Rumi in his book
    A Garden Beyond Paradise.
Yale University Press for citations from David Bentley Hart,
    The Experience of God: Being, Consciousness, Bliss.
From *The Collected Works of St. John of the Cross*, translated by Kieran
    Kavanaugh and Otilio Rodriguez Copyright © 1964, 1979, 1991 by
    Washington Province of Discalced Carmelites ICS Publications 2131
    Lincoln Road, N.E. Washington, DC 20002-1199 U.S.A.
    www.icspublications.org
Excerpts from #6 [21.], #14 [51.], #25 [61.], # 51 [91.] from *Tao Te Ching By
    Lao Tzu, A New English Version*, With Foreword And Notes, by Stephen
    Mitchell. Translation copyright © 1988 by Stephen Mitchell. Reprinted
    by permission of HarperCollins Publishers.

10 9 8 7 6 5 4 3 2 1

Homebound Publications greatly values the natural environment and invests
in environmental conservation. Our books are printed on paper with chain of
custody certification from the Forest Stewardship Council, Sustainable Forestry
Initiative, and the Program for the Endorsement of Forest Certification.

The Physics of Angels (with Rupert Sheldrake)

Confessions: The Making of a Post-Denominational Priest

Illuminations of Hildegard of Bingen

*Occupy Spirituality: A Radical Vision
For a New Generation (with Adam Bucko)*

Creation Spirituality: Liberating Gifts for the Peoples of the Earth

One River, Many Wells: Wisdom Springing from Global Faiths

*Sheer Joy: Conversations with Thomas Aquinas
on Creation Spirituality*

*Sins of the Spirit, Blessings of the Flesh:
Transforming Evil in Soul and Society*

*Hildegard of Bingen, A Saint for Our Times:
Unleashing Her Power in the 21st Century*

Hildegard of Bingen's Book of Divine Works, Songs and Letters

Western Spirituality: Historical Roots, Ecumenical Routes

*Wrestling with the Prophets:
Essays on Creations Spirituality and Everyday Life*

*Whee! We, Wee All the Way Home:
Toward a Prophetic, Sensual Spirituality*

*The Pope's War: Why Ratzinger's Secret Crusade
Has Imperiled the Church and What Can Be Saved*

Meditations with Meister Eckhart

I happily and gratefully dedicate this book to my teaching colleagues at the University of Creation Spirituality over the years who have passed on and are now among the ancestors. Included are M. C. Richards, Sister Jose Hobday, Jeremy Taylor, Robert Rice, Buck Ghosthorse, Rolf Osterberg, Shanya Kirsten, Monsignor Bob Fox.

Contents

Part II: 9 Names for the God Without a Name
(*The Apophatic Divinity*)

Part III: Some Practices to Undergo Apropos of the Names of God Offered in this Book

Appendix: Aquinas on Names of God

Endnotes

God Has a Trillion Faces

THE ANCIENT *VEDAS* OF INDIA TELL US THAT "The One Existence the wise call by many names."

How many names for Divinity are there? Do the names for God change? Ought they change as humans evolve and as circumstances of life evolve around us? Are we among the "wise" that the Vedas speak of who are eager to call the One Existence by many names? Do we have permission—and maybe a serious responsibility—to change our understanding and naming of God as we mature as individuals and as we evolve as a species and as we face a critical time, a "turning time," in human and planetary history?

The great medieval mystic Meister Eckhart declared: "I pray God to rid me of God."

Apparently he was so convinced in the need to allow God and our names for God to evolve that he actually prayed to God to move on from being "God." He challenges us further when he declares: "The highest and loftiest thing that a person can let go of is to let go of God for the sake of God."

How many names for God have humans come up with? And which ones might serve us best today and what new ones beckon us? One answer to that question is a simple one: There are as many names for "God" as there are languages in the world, for each language calls God by a different word. Examples: God (English); Gott (German); Dieu (French); Dios (Spanish); Allah (Arabic); Gut (Norwegian); Theos (Greek); Deus (Portuguese); bog (Russian); Dia (Irish); Elohim (Hebrew); Marta (Polish); Kalou (Fijian), etc. etc.

But that is by no means the whole story. For one thing, each language may well have multiple words for "God." For example in English we can talk of Divinity; Spirit; Creator; Deity; Godhead; Goddess; and much more. If this is true in English no doubt it is true in other languages as well.

Every religion offers its name for the Divine: Brahmin; Krishna; Tao; Buddha; Tara; Allah; Yahweh; Adonai; Tagashala; Wankan Tanka; Oshun; Isis; Christ, to name a few.

So where else do we come up with alternative names or images of God? The Sacred Scriptures of the world are one such place; and the mystics of the world are another; and science is another. The Muslim tradition boasts a powerful practice of reciting the "99 Most Beautiful Names" of God and in many ways that practice has inspired this short book wherein I present 89 current names for Divinity that I think are most beautiful and wonderful and useful for our times. I am grateful for that Muslim practice to which I am indebted and which I have often prayed myself.

The ancient scriptures of Hinduism known as the *Bhagavad Gita* tell us this: "God has a million faces." St Thomas Aquinas, medieval theologian and mystic, goes even further. He says that every being is a name for God when he says: "Even the very ones who were experienced concerning Divinity, such as the apostles and prophets, praise God as the Cause of all things from the many things caused." Aquinas, in this amazing passage, goes on to name 49 names for God that sixth century Syrian monk Dennis the Areopagite found in Scripture alone and discussed in his foundational work, *The Divine Names*. What follows from his statement is that there are literally multiple trillions upon trillions upon trillions of names for God. Countless creatures—therefore, countless faces, countless names. But at the end of his treatise (which I reproduce as an Appendix in this book) he says no being is a name for God because "God surpasses all things."

If there are trillions upon trillions of names for God, who am I, and who are you, the reader of this book, to dare to choose only 89? Well, first of all, this book is unfinished. It is open ended and that is why the last pages of each section are left blank so you may add your own most wonderful and useful names for God. Secondly, while there may be trillions upon trillions of names for God, it is clear that we humans are limited. We can only take so much input and reflect deeply on a very finite number of thoughts and concepts and names. So this book presents a very finite number, *a working number,* of possible names for God. Hopefully they might prove useful and inspire other useful names from the reader.

In this book I seek to offer a finite number of names for God that I sense might be useful for us in the difficult "in-between" times in which we find ourselves at this dawning of the post-modern era.

I include a modest meditation with each name to assist a kind of "unraveling" and unpacking of each name. I invite the reader to deepen the experience by his/her own meditation and investigation. Some have called our times "apocalyptic" and philosopher Theodore Richards points out that "apocalypse" also means "revelation." Perhaps, in dire times, deeper mysteries are revealing themselves, unveiling themselves, to us. But we need to listen deeply. We need to develop our muscles of contemplation. We need to cease projecting and to learn anew to let go so that we can listen truthfully to the "hidden Word" of silence. From this hidden place of silence, this "cave of the heart" as Father Bede Griffiths calls it, might emerge some new and fresh language for a spiritual awakening, for rich names for Divinity, for a global renaissance. Hopefully, this short book can assist that important task.

As humans undergo deep changes, so too does our understanding of God or Divinity. Both Meister Eckhart, a medieval mystic activist, and Alfred North Whitehead, a twentieth century scientific philosopher, agree that Divinity evolves. "God becomes where all creatures express God," notes Eckhart. Thus, our names for God increase in possibilities and evolve as evolution continues all around us. Deepak Chopra sees God's evolution this way: "What actually evolved was human understanding....We think that God changes, because our own perception waxes and wanes. The messages keep coming though and God keeps showing different faces....As awareness evolves, so does God. This journey never ends."

Which, among the trillions upon trillions of God-names might serve us the best today? And serve the planet the best? And therefore serve God the best? That is the question that this book is presenting. Hopefully, it will be useful, for as Aquinas insisted, a "little knowledge about important things is far more important than a lot of knowledge about unimportant things." A fresh understanding and language about Divinity may assist us to come up with fresh understandings of ourselves and thus the societies and institutions we feel called to give birth to as we struggle to assist other species to survive and to survive ourselves, to be sustainable, even to thrive and become beautiful and worthy of our holy existence.

Meister Eckhart warns us that when we talk about God we stutter and stumble. This is important

In Part II we pick out 9 names of the apophatic Divinity, the Unnameable Divinity. The word "apophatic" means "drawn to the dark." Coming out of an age called the "Enlightenment," many people today are unfamiliar with this category of God-naming that denies any name for God but rests with the experience that God surpasses all naming. In the same amazing passage where Aquinas talks about how every creature is a name for God he ends his discourse this way: "And the Divine One is none of these beings insofar as God surpasses all things." So clearly he is urging us to name God broadly— but also to back off from any naming. Eckhart puts it this way: "All creatures want to express God in all their works; let them all speak, coming as close as they can, they still cannot speak him. Whether they want to or not...they all want to speak God and he still remains unspoken." Thus we speak God and we fail to speak God. God is spoken and unspoken. There is paradox here, there is an invitation to see and not to see, to recognize and to let go. When it comes to things spiritual, paradox is always a good thing. It strikes at the heart of our compulsions to control. It also invites humor in and defuses temptations to excessive literalism and religious zealotry and idolatry, which gives birth to rigid fundamentalisms.

In our time when much of God talk can be cheapened by bad religion and outright idolatry of false gods (avarice, racism, militarism, might-makes-right, excessive nationalism among them), it is especially valuable and important to consider the apophatic naming of Divinity. Divine names do not sit tidily in our left brains amidst definitions, numbers, dogmas and doctrines. As Augustine put it, "if you comprehend it, it is not God." Also, when dark matter and dark energy and black holes characterize the scientific parlance of our time, the God of darkness may be emerging with a special role to play at this time in history. We want to leave room for that surely. This we do in Part II.

In Part III we offer some exercises that might deepen the experience of reading and meditating on this book.

In a challenging and provocative study by Nancy Ellen Abrams, co-author of *The View from the Center of the Universe*, the author has this to say about contemporary God talk: "Our thinking about God today is like a potted plant that's root-bound and can barely grow. The pot is made of old metaphors, images, and stories. Not only are science and spirituality not necessarily antagonistic but science may be the only way to break out of the pot and put our spiritual roots into Earth and the cosmos, where they can grow freely. Where they can be coherent with reality."

Abrams is not trying to throw God out of the picture—quite the opposite, she insists that while science can help define good and evil, "defining the good" doesn't necessarily make it happen; we all know that science has also enabled terrible things on enormous scales. We need our god-capacity to generate the spiritual power—the motivation, trust, and faith in each other—to bring good about. How we conceive of God will have enormous impact on how we behave toward each other, how we justify our actions, what we believe is possible, and what we find sacred and are therefore willing to sacrifice to protect….We need a new understanding of God. We need a God that can connect us spiritually to the real universe and guide our now globally conscious species toward a long-term and honorable civilization.

Perhaps this book might contribute to stirring imaginations for a new understanding of God. I hope it does and that the reader reads it in a meditative way for that is how it was intended. Let your heart and intuitive brain ride along with the images and names presented herein.

Finally, I celebrate the excellent work by David Bentley Hart, an eastern Orthodox philosopher, who in a more didactic study than this one is also on a quest for a more useable naming of Divinity. In his important book, *The Experience of God: Being, Consciousness, Bliss*, he offers some wise observations to the topic at hand when he warns that God-talk can get easily muddled by mushy religious thinking.

Any debate over an intelligent designer, or a supreme being within space and time who merely supervises history and legislates morals, or a demiurge whose operations could possibly be rivals of the physical causes describable by scientific cosmology…most definitely has nothing whatsoever to do with the God worshipped in the great theistic religions, or described in their philosophical traditions, or reasoned toward by their deepest logical reflections upon the contingency of the world.

He encourages us to leave seventeenth-century deism and eighteenth-century 'natural history' aside today. His diagnosis of what ails us religiously is this: "The reason the very concept of God has become at once so impoverished, so thoroughly mythical, and ultimately so incredible for so many modern persons is not because of all the interesting things we have learned over the past few centuries, but because of all the vital things we have forgotten. Above all, somehow, we have as a culture forgotten being: the self-evident mystery of existence...." How has this happened? "Perhaps that is attributable not only to how we have been taught to think, but how we have been taught to live. Late modernity is, after all, a remarkably shrill and glaring reality, a dazzling chaos of the beguilingly trivial and terrifyingly atrocious, a world of ubiquitous mass media and constant interruption, an interminable spectacle whose only unifying theme is the imperative to acquire and spend." We have little time to reflect "upon the mystery that manifests itself not as a thing among other things, but as the silent event of being itself." In our "quest to master beings," we have ventured very far indeed away from being.

That this book might bring us closer to the mystery of being and the mystery beyond mystery is my hope. That it may loosen the doors that hold us back from trusting our own deep experience of the God of mystery is my prayer.

Matthew Fox
Vallejo, California
December 21, 2017
Winter solstice, my 77th birthday and the day of the launching of the Order of the Sacred Earth

PART I

80 Most Wonderful and Useful Names for God

The Cataphatic Divinity

To call God love can really be quite shocking since many people, in invoking the name of God, think of Judge or Potentate or stern Father or indifferent unmoved mover or cause of Fate. But that "God is love" represents a profoundly alternative direction for humankind. What kind of love? Love of forests? Of music? Of eating? Of children? Of lovers? The word "love" is such a broad word, especially in English, that it applies to so many things. But to say God is love is to render God omni-present, omni-felt, part of everyday life—and of every day aspiration. For who does not aspire for love? To give love and to receive love? How great is love, how vast, how without limitation? Do all creatures love in some way?

Just today I read the story of a wounded dog, a Doberman named Khan, who after just four days into a new and adopted family with a 17-month-old baby saved that baby's life by suddenly picking it up by its diaper and tossing it across the yard. At first the bystanders thought the dog was attacking the baby—until they realized the dog took sick very suddenly. Rushing it to the veterinarian they learned he had been bitten by one of the most venomous snakes on the planet—the Mulga—and Khan was near death for days as the vets struggled to save its life. Instead of killing the baby the dog saved its life, had intervened when he saw the snake approaching the tiny child, and put its own life on the line. As it turned out the dog lived. And the child too. Love among the animals. This too is love, this too is God present.

2.

God Is Goodness

JULIAN OF NORWICH TELLS US that "I saw that God is everything that is good and energizing…. and the goodness that everything possesses is God." If she is correct and all beings carry goodness, is this another way of experiencing the omnipresence of God—God as the goodness in all things? God is the goodness within goodness. Our experiences of goodness then constitute our experiences of God. We need to be hunter-gatherers after goodness therefore.

Meister Eckhart, when asked how you know a good person, responds: "A good person praises good people." To praise is to recognize goodness—and rejoice at it by celebrating it. We need to become hunter-gatherers for praise. Aquinas teaches that God "is sheer goodness" and is "the fount of all goodness" and since goodness of itself is generous, "God is supremely good and therefore supremely generous." Hart concurs: "The good is nothing less than God himself, in his aspect as the original source and ultimate end of all desire: that transcendent reality in which all things exist and in which the will has its highest fulfillment….Our longing for the good is an aboriginal longing for God."

3.

God Is the One to Whom
We Give Our Thanks

IF WE ARE SURROUNDED by goodness and take goodness in so as to praise it where we find it, then we are urged to give thanks for life, for existence, for the goodness tasted therein. When Dorothy Day, an atheist and communist at the time, became pregnant she was so overcome by the beauty of bearing a new living being inside her that she converted to Christianity. Why? "Because I had to give thanks to someone," she said. God is the One to whom we render our Thanks.

We need to make a simple return, Hart says, "to that original apprehension of the gratuity of all things" a deep response that is not neutral but that is grateful to "the limitless beauty of being, which is to say, upon the beauty of being seen as a gift that comes from beyond all possible beings." Thomas Aquinas considers gratitude to be the very essence of healthy religion: to be religious is to be thankful. One is never half-full of thanks—one is *thank-full.*

4.

God Is Existence, Being and *Isness*

ECKHART SAYS "GOD IS BEING" And a "fountain of being" and Aquinas says: "God is pure existence....God is essential existence and all other things are beings by participation." Deepak Chopra writes: "God is not a mythical person—he is Being itself." He elaborates: "The vast physical mechanism we call the universe behaves more like a mind than like a machine. How did mind ever find a way to manifest as the physical world?...The very fact that *anything* exists is supernatural—literally beyond the rules of the natural world." The true miracle is existence itself.

Hart underscores the uniqueness and the necessity of God as being when he observes that "all physical reality is contingent upon some cause of being as such, since existence is not an intrinsic physical property, and since no physical reality is logically necessary." He recognizes that "the ultimate source of existence cannot be some item or event that has long since passed away or concluded, like a venerable ancestor or even the Big Bang itself—either of which is just another contingent physical entity or occurrence—but must be a constant wellspring of being, at work even now." Aquinas holds the very same perspective when he says: "God's work whereby God brings things into being must not be taken as the work of a craftsman who makes a box and then leaves it. For God continues to give being." Indeed, God "continually pours out existence into things." Rabbi Heschel concurs when he says Creation "is not an act that happened once upon a time, once and for ever. The act of bringing the world into existence is a continuous process. God called the world into being, and that call goes on....Every instant is an act of creation."

Hart makes a stern judgment about our culture when he declares that we are out of touch with being: we "may well be the social order that has ventured furthest away from being in its quest to master beings." The specialness of the divine Being and its relationship to being resides in the fact that "nothing within the cosmos contains the ground of its own being." Because "it is far easier to think about beings than about being as such....we therefore always risk losing sight of the mystery of being behind the concepts we impose upon it."

Eckhart defines creation as "the giving of being" and says that "Isness is God." He is saying that all being is a representation of Divinity. This would echo Aquinas' teaching that "to exist is the most perfect thing of all, for compared to existence, everything else is potential."

5.

God Is the Ground of Being

DIVINITY IS TO BE FOUND in the depth of things, the foundation of things, the profundity of things. We all have a depth, a ground, a presence and there, says Eckhart, lies Divinity, for God is the ground of being and "God's ground is my ground and my ground is God's ground." Thich Nhat Hanh agrees when he says, "all notions applied to the phenomenal worlds…are transcended. The greatest relief we can obtain is available when we touch the ultimate, 'Tillich's 'ground of being'.…Life is no longer confined to time and space." Thich Nhat Hanh equates "nirvana" and "God" and "ground of being" when he says: "God as the ground of being cannot be conceived of. Nirvana also cannot be conceived of. If we are aware when we use the word 'nirvana' or the word 'God' that we are talking about the ground of being there is no danger in using these words."

6.

God Is the Cause of Wonder

BEING IS NOT JUST a fact or a thing. Being fills us with wonder for there is an "immense preciousness of being," says Rabbi Heschel, which "is not an object of analysis but a cause of wonder." Heschel asks: "Who lit the wonder before our eyes and the wonder of our eyes?" We become struck by an "unmitigated wonder" and we ask about the universe: "Who could believe it? Who could conceive it?" And "How shall we ever reciprocate for breathing and thinking, for sight and hearing, for love and achievement?" Because of being, an "awareness of the divine…intrudes first as a sense of wonder."

Einstein concurs when he says: "There is no true science which does not emanate from the mysterious. Every thinking person must be filled with wonder and awe just by looking up at the stars." Awe moves us beyond knowledge to wisdom. Aquinas observes that what the scientist, the poet and the philosopher all share in common is this: Each "is concerned with the marvelous." Indeed, "amazement (*admiratio*) is the beginning of philosophy and science" and "one meditates on creation in order to view and marvel at divine wisdom."

7.

God Is the Mind of the Universe

AT THE CONCLUSION of his ground-breaking book, *The Self-Organizing Universe*, physicist Erich Jantsch asserts: "God is...the mind of the universe." He defines "mind" as "self-organization dynamics at many levels, as a dynamics which itself evolves. In this respect, all natural history is also history of mind." Jantsch draws an accurate conclusion when he compares the paradigm of self-organization in science with the experience of the mystics over the ages: "This connectedness of our own life processes with the dynamics of an all embracing universe has so far been accessible only to mystic experience. In the synthesis, it becomes part of science which in this way comes closer to life."

Where and Who is God in all this? Jantsch continues: "The divine, however, becomes manifest neither in personal nor any other form, but in the total evolutionary dynamics of a multilevel reality. Instead of the numinous, we may also speak of meaning. Each of us would then, in Aldous Huxley's terms, 'be Mind-at-large' and share in the evolution of this all-embracing mind and thus also in the divine principle, in meaning.... The God-idea does not stand above and outside of evolution as an ethical norm, but in true mysticism is placed into the unfolding and self-realization of evolution."

If God is the "mind" of the universe, we should remember that "mind" is not without heart or love. Mind is inclusive of love wherever we see mind at work.

8.

God Is Evolution
and Pure Potential

JANTSCH MAINTAINS THAT GOD abandons himself many
times in a sequence of evolution in which he transforms
himself. God is thus "not absolute, he evolves himself—
he *is evolution*. Since we have called the self-organizing
dynamics of a system its mind, we may now say that
God is not the creator, but the mind of the universe." The
"'God-structure' is neither form nor quantity, but the
non-unfolded, the totality of undifferentiated qualities.
It is pure potential."

This last point is especially striking since in the
Aristotelian tradition adapted by Thomas Aquinas God
is called "pure act." The idea of God as "pure potential"
indicates some feminist influence in tapering down
mere Yang energy with some Yin energy. It holds up
the Creative and Motherly dimension to Divinity in a
special way.

9.

God Is
the Planetary Mind Field

DR. ARNE A. WYLLER, professor of Astrophysics at the Royal Swedish Academy, in his book, *The Planetary Mind*, calls God a "Planetary Mind Field." What is this Mind Field? "To me, the Mind Field resides in a mental energy field suffused throughout the entire Earth—the visual manifestation of which may be the life forms created. But those life forms live and die independently of the Mind Field, thrown out into the cruel Darwinian world of natural selection and adaptation." For Wyller this Field is "not all-powerful. It is itself evolving in its creativity, and it is restrained to conform to existing physical laws in its biological creativity." He likes to "identify with a higher intelligence that is restricted, maybe even fallible: the Planetary Mind Field."

Having computed his mathematical reckoning, Wyller is convinced that chance does not explain the existence of life in all its complexity. "The Darwinists and neo-Darwinists have never been able to use hard mathematical calculations based on probability theory to uphold the assertion that chance could realistically be the creative agent. The words of highly respected biologist George Wald, 'Given so much time the impossible becomes possible, the possible probable and the probable virtually certain,' simply do not suffice anymore." The molecular process underlying protein synthesis is "inexplicably complex" as the classic work *Molecular Biology of the Cell* puts it. Just to build the DNA instructions for a simple protein "made up of only thirty-four amino acids through chance encounters in a primordial broth would in all probability take far more time than the age of the Universe."

10.

God Is a Playing Intelligence

WYLLER PROPOSES THAT A sense of fun and play ought to be applied to the Mind Field because "in the development of evolution we see an evolving, playing intelligence slowly maturing to the point of creating humankind—a *Deus ludens* (God playing)." Maybe God is a trickster after all.

Wyller recognizes the unconscious in each human being as a "communication channel" to the Mind Field, and vice versa. The human mind is still young and holds a tenuous link to the Mind Field although mystics have shown the way. The Mind Field itself is all about love. As Wyller sees it, "Nature around us bespeaks of its love, and the voices of the mystics—be they from Greece, Western Europe, India, or China—echo through history: God is Love." Wyller anticipates that "the number of mystics grows as evolution progresses in perfecting our communication with the Mind Field."

11.

God Is Creative Intelligence that Operates by Way of Evolution

DEEPAK CHOPRA NAMES GOD as "the intelligence that conceives, governs, constructs, and becomes the universe." Is this teaching in harmony both with science and with inherited titles for Divinity? It would seem it is. That God has chosen evolution as the way to birth, govern and construct the universe is becoming clearer and clearer thanks to science. As we saw above, that God "becomes the universe" is spoken to by great mystics like Meister Eckhart who says that God becomes as the universe and creation become.

Evolution is very real however; it is the *means* by which Intelligence conceives, governs, constructs the universe. Teilhard de Chardin rhapsodizes about evolution as his calling or holy vocation when he writes: "That magic word 'evolution' which haunted my thoughts like a tune: which was to me like unsatisfied hunger, like a promise held out to me, like a summons to be answered."

12.

God Is the One in Whom We Live, Move and Have Our Being

THAT GOD IS "the one in whom we live, move and have our being" (Acts 17.28) is a classic statement on panentheism (God in us and we in God)—and it is significant that it comes so early in the history of the Christian movement. There are other examples too in the Christian Scriptures such as John speaking of the Father dwelling in us and we in God, Christ in us and we in Christ. And of course among the mystics there are myriad examples of panentheism including Mechtild of Magdeburg telling us that the day of her spiritual awakening was the day she saw and knew she saw "all things in God and God in all things." Like fish in water, the water is in us and we are in the water. Eckhart says that "ignorant people falsely imagine" that creation exists "outside of God." Instead, God is "round about us completely enveloping us."

14.

God Is the Unity of All Things

THE JEWISH AND ISLAMIC TRADITIONS agree that God is One. Is oneness also God? Rabbi Heschel declares: "There is only one synonym for God: One." In many ways, the experience of oneness and unity is the very meaning of a mystical experience. Albert Einstein, in talking about the need for a "cosmic religion," said that "this oneness of creation, to my sense, is God."

Not only is God one but humans undergo "oneing" with God. Julian of Norwich talks about the "beautiful oneing" that takes place in the human soul that "is known and loved from without beginning and in its creation oned to the Creator." Our oneing goes way back in time for "in our creation we were knit and oned to God. By this we are kept as luminous and noble as when we were created. By the force of this precious oneing we love, seek, praise, thank and endlessly enjoy our Creator." For Julian the great oneing applies to all of creation, it is cosmic in its scope. "I saw a great oneing between Christ and us because when he was in pain we were in pain. All creatures of God's creation that can suffer pain suffered with him. The sky and the earth failed at the time of Christ's dying because he too was part of nature."

Rumi also sings of oneing:

> I know nothing of two worlds—
> All I know is the One—
> I seek only One,
> I know only One,
> I find only One,
> And I sing of only One.

Eckhart declares that "we should sink eternally from something to nothing into this One."

15.

God Is Reality

THE SUFI TRADITION NAMES God as *al-Haqq*: Reality as such, underlying everything. While our being is wholly contingent, [God's] is necessary. God cannot not be, while we can not be. Hart maintains that God "is not a being but is at once 'beyond being' (in the sense that he transcends the totality of existing things) and also absolute 'Being itself' (in the sense that he is the source and ground of all thing)." God is "the reality that is present in all things as the very act of their existence." God for Hart is an "unconditioned reality (which, by definition, cannot be temporal or spatial or in any sense finite) upon which all else depends; otherwise nothing could exist at all."

Deepak Chopra asks this question: "What if God is reality? Only then would we be free from illusion. If you reduce God to a mental construct, you are stepping into illusion and its many aspects." Then he answers his question this way: "I apply the same standards to God that we ordinarily apply to reality. Reality doesn't come and go. It doesn't abandon us. What changes is how we relate to it…..Reality leads everyone forward. In the interval between birth and death, we all come to grips with reality; therefore, consciously or not, we are coming to grips with God."

16.

God Is the Enfolding and Unfolding of Everything That Is

FIFTEENTH CENTURY MYSTIC and scientist Nicolas of Cusa says: "the absolute, Divine Mind, is all that is in everything that is....Divinity is the enfolding and unfolding of everything that is." Divinity is the "universal form of being."

17.

God Is the Universe

DEEPAK CHOPRA SAYS "There is only God. The universe is God made manifest." Thomas Berry tells us that the Universe is the "primary sacred reality" and that we recover a sense of the sacred "only if we appreciate the universe beyond ourselves as a revelatory experience of that numinous presence whence all things come into being." This is how we become sacred ourselves, "by our participation in this more sublime dimension of the world about us." Moreover, "the universe is the primary revelation of the divine, the primary scripture, the primary locus of divine-human communion."

If any being qualifies as a name for God, then surely the greatest being of all, the universe itself, is in some way God. Aquinas observes: "Not only are individual creatures images of God but so too is the whole cosmos. God has produced a work in which the divine likeness is clearly reflected—I mean by this, the world itself."

What is at the heart of the universe? "Celebration," says Thomas Berry. "It is all an exuberant expression of existence itself."

18.

God Is the Self of the Universe

DEEPAK CHOPRA CALLS GOD "the self of the universe."
How is God the "self of the universe?" All beings have
a self, an inner existence. Hildegard of Bingen says: "no
creature, whether visible or invisible, lacks an interior
life." Does the universe as a whole have the same? Why
wouldn't it? *Is the universe an "I am"?* Humans have
given this cosmic selfhood many names: *Cosmic Christ;
Primordial Man; Buddha Nature; Image of God* among
them. (See #73)

19.

God Is the Newest and Youngest Thing in the Universe

IN THE ANCIENT *VEDAS* from India, God is called "most youthful." Meister Eckhart says that "God is novissimus," meaning the newest and youngest thing there is in the universe. He also says that "when we say God is eternal we mean God is eternally young." There is something youthful and "in the beginning" about God—this is why both the Hebrew Bible and the Christian Bible (John 1.1) begin with the words "In the beginning…." To return to the beginning is to return to God therefore. And we do return to the beginning, to our "unborn selves," as Eckhart puts it, and to the person you were before you were born. Buddhism too talks of recovering our "original face" which we possessed before we were born.

20.

God Is the Ancient One
of Ancient Days,
the "One Beyond Time"

NOT ONLY IS DIVINITY YOUNG and youngest; it is also ancient and before time; and beyond time. Eckhart says: "God is eternity" who dwells in "the fullness of time. There everything is present and new." But what is eternity? "Eternity is the peculiarity that being and being young are one." Because "both newness and life are proper to God," our dwelling in the eternal now is dwelling in newness and life, vitality and the source of energy.

Hart says that "God is eternal, not in the sense of possessing limitless duration but in the sense of transcending time altogether. Time is the measure of finitude, of change, of the passage from potentiality to actuality. God, however, being infinite actual being, is necessarily...the One beyond time, comprehending all times within his eternal 'now.'" We have glimpses of this "eternal now" when we undergo mystical experiences in moments of creativity or of great joy and ecstasy. At such times the past and future come together in the deep present and they are often accompanied by a deep Presence and a suspension of time—"Where did the time go?" we ask. This deep Presence *can also communicate as a very ancient presence.*

21.

God Is Energy

THICH NHAT HANH WRITES: "We know the Holy Spirit as energy and not as notions and words" and he calls the Holy Spirit "the energy of God in us, the true door." What shall we say about Energy? Does anything exist without it? Is Energy the force, the power, the creative goings on in every being in the universe? Is energy also the relationship, the networks, the interconnectivity in action between all beings as they relate to one another?

Meister Eckhart's observation that "God is a great underground river that no one can damn up and no one can stop" may be the ultimate metaphor in naming God as Energy. God is the unstoppable energy of all beings, a boundless source that cannot be slowed down or ultimately overcome. Energy upon energy, energy within energy. But Divinity works underground, in secret, in the dark, not readily accessible, one must hunt and search for such an underground river as this. One must dig a well to access this energy. Also, being "underground" is a feminine image of Divinity, God embedded in the Earth, not in the sky. A God of below, not just the above. A God from the deep, from the depth, from the underground.

Is this understanding of God as energy a new take on God as "unmoved mover," that is as the primary source of the universe's energy? Are energy and matter convertible as Einstein proposed in his equation $E=mc^2$? Convertible and interchangeable? What does that say of God?

22.

God Is Spirit

THE SCRIPTURES DECLARE THAT "The Spirit of the Lord fills the whole earth." (Wis 1.7) One does not see Spirit. Yet it is everywhere. One does not see wind either (only its results); or gravity; or attraction; or air; or breath. However, one experiences all these things. They are real. They too are reality. We see their effects when present and when absent. And they are important. Who are we without breath? Without air? Without gravity? Spirit "blows where it will" (John 3.8) and we pick up on it. Spirit and Wind and Air and Breath are the same words in many languages of the world.

24.

God Is the Within of Things

GOD IS THE WITHIN OF THINGS. Meister Eckhart says "it is proper to God...to be within, to be innermost." And John of the Cross says "the soul's center is God." When Chopra talks of the "self of the universe," he seems close to calling God the "within of things," or what Meister Eckhart calls the "innermost" dimension of things—in this case the *within* of the universe. We can rightly say that God is the light within light; the life within life; the joy within joy; the justice within justice; the unity within unity; the beauty within beauty; the desire within desire, the darkness within darkness, the silence within silence, the compassion within compassion and the self within selves.

25.

God Is Consciousness

Our capacity to think, reflect, ask questions, become aware and more aware, expand awareness, all this is consciousness. Is all this God? Is God our awareness—including our awareness and experience of God? Psychologist R. D. Laing thought this; he felt that "God is our experience of God." Deepak Chopra says: "God is pure consciousness, the source of all thoughts, feelings, and sensations." What is consciousness? "Consciousness is creative and intelligent. It can correlate a quadrillion brain connections or the fifty processes that a liver cell performs. It can keep track of simultaneous activities at the same time (allowing one to breathe, digest, walk, be pregnant, think about your baby, and feel happy at the same time). You are finding God whenever any of these aspects begins to expand. God enters everyday life this way."

Hart proposes that it may well be that "the fullness of being upon which all contingent beings depend is at the same time a limitless act of consciousness." Our rich inner lives of experience and thought are very real to us and "the source and ground of the mind's unity is the transcendent reality of unity as such, the simplicity of God, the one ground of both consciousness and being." God is "infinite consciousness" and therefore "perfect bliss."

Biologist Rupert Sheldrake asks whether we humans are wired "to connect with a mind or consciousness vastly greater than our own," and whether our minds "are of the same nature as the ultimate consciousness that underlies the universe." He is convinced that all religions—from Hinduism and Buddhism to Islam and Sikhism to Judaism and Christianity—teach us that we indeed connect to the source of consciousness, the Great Consciousness of the universe. He also believes that this is what most distinguishes the scientific materialist from the spiritual seeker: That for the former all consciousness is found exclusively in the human brain—never beyond it and never in other creatures. In such a worldview consciousness "ought not to exist. Materialism's problem is that consciousness does exist....Even to discuss consciousness presupposes that we are conscious ourselves." Consciousness is something far larger than our physical brains and even than ourselves.

26.

God Is Joy

AQUINAS TEACHES THAT "God is supremely joyful and therefore supremely conscious." Thus God's (and our) consciousness is relative to our joy—joy gives birth to awareness, to aliveness, to consciousness therefore. Also, joy belongs intimately to God according to Aquinas because "Sheer Joy is God's and this demands companionship." Joy also gives birth to community and to friendship, to companionship of all kinds. One wants to share joy. God does and we are driven to do the same.

In the East this joy is called *Ananda* or bliss which has been described as "the vibrancy of creation, the underlying dynamism that enters the world as vitality, desire, ecstasy, and joy." According to Deepak Chopra, "God is pure bliss, the source of every human joy."

27.

God Is Laughter

WE LAUGH WITH JOY and we laugh with paradox. God does, too, according to Eckhart who says: "When God laughs at the soul and the soul laughs back at God, the persons of the Trinity are begotten." Furthermore, "God takes sheer delight and laughter over a good deed," says Eckhart—those that result in justice-making especially. Activist and mystic Kristal Parks replaces the word "the big bang" as marking the origin of the universe with the "Great Guffaw." She thinks creation is born of a great cosmic laugh as she invokes Thomas Berry who says: "The Universe, throughout its vast extent in space and throughout its sequence of transformations in time, is a single multiform, celebrative event."

Are we celebrating?

28.

God Is Co-Creator,
and the Power of Creation

A CO-CREATOR CREATES with and alongside us and with and alongside all the other beings that unfold in the universe from mitochondria to galaxies and supernovas and black holes. Aquinas suggests that the same Spirit that hovered over the waters at the beginning of creation (today's creation story would say 'hovered over the fireball at the beginning of creation') hovers over the mind of the artist at work. When we are employing our intelligence and our creativity we are co-creating. Thomas Merton called this the work of the Holy Spirit.

Scientists Jantsch and Wyller above seem to see it that way as well, God and all of Nature co-creating, God and humans co-creating. Arthur Rubenstein put it this way: "I have noticed through experience and through my own observations that Providence, Nature, God, or what I would call the Power of Creation, seems to favor human beings who accept and love life unconditionally. And I am certainly one who does, with all my heart."

God is a Creator and Co-creator but we require trust to contribute our share to the joint work.

Furthermore, though we are a powerful (and therefore dangerous) species, a bit of humility is in order since, as Wyller points out, "The inescapable fact is that during the 99.9 percent of biological evolutionary time on Earth, God—as symbolized in human religions—was not involved in the affairs of humans, because humans were not yet created."

29.

God Is Greening Power

CELTIC POET DYLAN THOMAS WRITES: "The force that through the green fuse drives the flower/Drives my green age;....The force that drives the water through the rocks /Drives my red blood." This Celtic appreciation for a driving green force is found centuries earlier in Hildegard of Bingen who lived in a Celtic monastery in Germany. She invented a word in Latin, *viriditas*, or "greening power." She attributes Greening Power to the Holy Spirit and sees "all verdant greening, all creativity" throughout creation. Indeed, she identifies it with the Word who "manifests itself in every creature" as well as with human creativity which "contains all moistness, all verdancy, all germinating powers. It is in so many ways fruitful. All creation comes from it."

We are to participate with the divine greening power by remaining "wet and green and moist and juicy"—like the rest of creation is. We are a people who "were meant to green," but when we destroy nature by our neglect or greed we displace creativity with "shriveled barrenness."

31.

God, the Holy Spirit, Is a Rushing River

MEISTER ECKHART CALLS THE Holy Spirit a "rushing river" and a "divine river" that is eager to fill us on a regular basis and "causes us to rejoice." The image of a rushing river connotes wetness, newness, power and freshness and in Eckhart's words it "springs," "rises," "presses," and "leaps." Indeed, "living waters will flow" from our good deeds, he declares. "Fountains of living water" are spoken of in John's gospel—"If any person is thirsty, let him come to me," shouts Jesus. (Jn 7.38).

Who is not thirsty? Who is not dry at times and seeking some wet nourishment? Is the rushing river the energy of creativity that comes over all of us as co-creators, the power of the Creative Spirit, whom Eckhart calls the "Transformer," at work?

32.

God Is Flow

I KNOW A YOUNG PHYSICIST who is very taken with studying synchronicity and also with the concept of *Flow*. So much so that he has referred to God as "Flow." One of his favorite books is a study of Flow by Mihaly Csikszentmihalyi in which he speaks of flow this way: Consciousness becomes "unusually well ordered" when thoughts, intensions, feelings and all the senses are focused on the same goal. Experience is in harmony. This leads to "ecstasy, to self-fulfillment" and work becomes "purposeful and enjoyable." What is called "optimal experience" occurs when people are so involved in an activity that nothing else seems to matter; the "experience itself is so enjoyable that people will do it even at great cost, for the sheer sake of doing it." He found this to be a universal experience with people interviewed around the world.

Aquinas calls God an "unfailing flow… a living fountain that is not diminished in spite of its continuous outflow."

33.

God Is Light

TODAY'S SCIENCE REMINDS US that "light is a vital ingredient in all atoms and in the molecules and life forms—including humans—that are made up of atoms....Light is by far the most preponderant particle in the Universe....Although most of the energy resides in matter, almost all particles in the Universe are those of light. If there is a meaningful scheme to things—and the speed of evolution argues that there must be—then light must somehow be a very important ingredient."

That God is light is one of the most universal names for God. We find it in the Christian Gospels—"I am the light of the world" (Jn 8:12) and mystics—Aquinas says "God is light; and one who approaches this light is illuminated, as Isaiah says: 'Rise, in love, and be enlightened.'" The Psalmist tells us that God comes "robed in a robe of light." (Ps 104:2) Hildegard says God is a "true light that gives light to all lights" and Christ the same and that we become flooded with this light.

God as Light is found in many other religions around the world. The Buddha talked of "enlightenment" and calls people to "be you lamps unto yourself" and we learn that "Krishna is the source of light in all luminous objects" and in the Vedas, Brahman is celebrated as Light: "The cosmic waters glow. I am Light!/ The light glows. I am Brahman!" In the *Mundaka Upanishad* we read: "Radiant in his light, yet invisible in the sacred place of the heart, the Spirit is the supreme abode wherein dwells all that moves and breathes and sees….He is self-luminous and more subtle than the smallest; From the Light of the Spirit, the sun, moon and stars give light; and his radiance illumines all Creation." It is this very great Light that is found within humans as well. "There is a light that shines above this heaven, above all worlds, above everything that exists in the highest worlds beyond which there are no higher—this is the Light that shines within man."

The monk Thomas Merton had an existential experience of this truth when, at noon rush hour in downtown Louisville, Kentucky, he saw the light in everyone busy on the street going to lunch. He wrote in his journal the next day: "How is it possible to tell everyone they are all walking around shining like the sun?"

34.

God, the Holy Spirit, Is Fire

THE HOLY SPIRIT is often depicted by the mystics as a kind of *fire*. Thus Hildegard of Bingen writes: "Who is the Holy Spirit? The Holy Spirit is a Burning Spirit. It kindles the hearts of humankind. Like tympanum and lyre it plays them, gathering volume in the temple of the soul." Meister Eckhart says that "God glows and burns with all the divine wealth and all the divine bliss in the spark of the soul" and is never extinguished there. Hidden in this spark is "something like the original outbreak of all goodness, something like a brilliant light that glows incessantly and something like a burning fire which burns incessantly. This fire is nothing other than the Holy Spirit."

In his poem, "The Living Flame of Love," John of the Cross describes what he calls the "total transformation of the soul in the Beloved" wherein God and soul produce a "living flame....This flame of love is the Holy Spirit [that] bathes the soul in glory and refreshes it with the quality of divine life." It follows that our work burns for "all the acts of the soul are divine" and "since love is never idle, but in continual motion, it is always emitting flames everywhere like a blazing fire."

35.

God Is Compassion

Thomas Aquinas says that "compassion is the fire that Jesus came to set on the earth." Rabbi Heschel says that "Humanity is a reminder of God. As God is compassionate, let humanity be compassionate." Meister Eckhart declares that "we can call God love, we can call God knowledge, but the best name for God is compassion." Compassion is our response to interdependence, to our interconnectivity, to our shared humanity, to our shared being-ness with other beings. Compassion is our living out of what Thich Naht Hanh calls our "interbeing."

Given that today's science holds interdependence and interconnectivity as foundations to all bodily and ecological relationships, it would seem that Eckhart has hit on something primal and profound: Our capacity for compassion. In the Jewish tradition compassion is the "secret" name for God. Jesus let this secret out of the bag in Luke 6:26: "Be you compassionate as your Creator in heaven is compassionate."

37.

God Is the Great Challenger
and the Ground of Conscience

RABBI HESCHEL CAUTIONS that it is not enough to have a regard for the Ground of Being. We must also have "concern for the unregarded." We are to be the hands of the divine compassion and it is our conscience that urges us. We respond to a divine challenge, a "challenging transcendence," to act out of love and concern for other beings. In this way we can say that God is the Ground of Conscience. If we are interdependent with all beings, then surely The Ground of Being challenges us to act on behalf of other beings by our caring deeply and by working fiercely for justice and compassion.

38.

God Is Life

OFTEN THE MYSTICS TALK about God as "Life." Aquinas says "God is the cause of all life" and "Divine life is per se alive,…supereminently alive…and ineffable." Howard Thurman tells us the "most wonderful fact of all" is that "life is alive!" Hildegard of Bingen, Meister Eckhart, and Julian of Norwich all celebrate God as Life. In my first book, written forty-five years ago, I defined prayer as a "radical response to life." I still abide by that understanding of prayer. It has worked meaningful results in my own life and in many others that I have witnessed.

The "radical" or root or deep response to life is a Yes (this is called mysticism); or a No (this is called prophecy—or standing up to injustice). We are all mystics and prophets called to respond to Life deeply and along the way of deep living.

39.

God Is the Beloved

THERE IS AN INTIMACY and even playfulness implied in calling God "the beloved" that great mystics like Rumi, John of the Cross and Julian of Norwich know and tell us about. What is more intimate and personal than one's "beloved"? Here is John of the Cross waxing on about God as Beloved.

> My Beloved is the mountains,
> And lonely wooded valleys,
> Strange islands,
> And resounding rivers,
> The whistling of love-stirring breezes,
> The tranquil night
> At the time of the rising dawn,
> Silent music.
> Sounding solitude,
> The supper that refreshes, and deepens love.

In this one poem John is naming numerous deep experiences we have in nature when we approach it in a sacred and receptive way—from mountains to valleys to islands to rivers to breezes to night to dawn to music and eating—so long as solitude accompanies us we can experience Divinity in nature. Indeed, creation becomes the kingdom of God, as we shall see below (#80).

Hildegard of Bingen declares: "Creation is allowed in intimate love to speak to the Creator as if to a lover." Thus the "beloved" relationship applies to all creatures. Julian of Norwich exclaims: "God wants to be thought of as our Lover." She elaborates: "The love of God makes such a unity in us that when we see this unity no one is able to separate oneself from another." She promises that "God will appear suddenly and joyfully to all lovers of God." Aquinas observes that "the lover is not content with superficial knowledge of the beloved, but strives for intimate discovery and even entering into the beloved."

Rumi speaks often of God as the Beloved. A Rumi scholar explains: "All a Sufi strives for, all he reaches for, all he ever wants is the Beloved. This unswerving love causes him to see the form of his Beloved everywhere: as pure beauty and pure love, as the master and the playful 'Friend,' as the vibrant, living presence that permeates every aspect of life… Union with the Beloved is the goal of all Sufi practice." Rumi exclaims,

Open your eyes! The Beloved,
Is staring you right in the face!

40.

God Is Beauty

THE MODERN ERA THREW out the word "Beauty" as a philosophical category much less an ethical one. However, that was not true of pre-modern thinkers. Eckhart says: "This then is salvation, to marvel at the beauty of created things…." Aquinas says God is a "fountain of total beauty" and "beauty itself beautifying all things." Indeed, God who is "supersubstantial beauty, is called beauty because God bestows beauty on all created beings." Hart observes that beauty "is wholly elusive of definition—it never makes sense to say, 'This is beautiful because…'—and yet it is inescapable in its force…. Beauty is gloriously useless; it has no purpose but itself." He cites Kabir who claims that all delight in beauty is adoration of God and Thomas Traherne who encourages us to "recognize creation as the mirror of God's infinite beauty."

Nicholas of Cusa calls Wisdom "a supreme and terrible beauty" that can unite people of all religious differences. The Sufi tradition declares: "God is beautiful and He loves beauty." The Navajo tradition offers prayers daily to the God of beauty such as this one: "I walk with beauty before me, I walk with beauty behind me, I walk with beauty above me, I walk with beauty below me, I walk with beauty all around me, your world is so beautiful O God."

41.

God Is Truth

To APPROACH TRUTH is to approach God. To seek truth is to seek God. The pursuit of truth is a godly act; it is a prayer. Study is a prayer provided that the goal is not ego-enhancement or fame or power but that a pure heart is brought to the project. This means the study of anything—stars or birds, mathematics or engineering, psychology or the origins of life, the mystics or politics—all of it is a journey to the Divine. Hart writes: "In God lies at once the deepest truth of mind and the most universal truth of existence, and that for this reason the world can truly be known by us." We all seek truth and we are all capable of finding some.

Our yearning for truth is deeper than ethics, as Rumi observes:

> They say you bring the word of God
> Yet all I hear is talk of good and bad—
> Nothing of love or truth.

And again, "Beyond the teachings of right and wrong there lies a field. I will meet you there." God is a field of Truth, the field where we encounter truth and truth encounters us. *The Bhagavad Gita* declares that a world without truth is a world without God and in such a world desire alone will rule.

42.

God Is Music

HILDEGARD OF BINGEN, who was a musical innovator and genius as a musician, asks:

> Who is the Trinity?
> You are music.
> you are life.
> Source of everything,
> Creator of everything.

Music speaks, or better sings, deeply to most everyone's soul. For Hildegard, it is invariably God doing the singing and harmonizing.

Nor is she alone. Aboriginal accounts and Hindu accounts of creation talk of primal sounds and song as being the origin of the universe (the Christian "Logos" is a "Word" or sound as well). Planets with their elliptical orbits and the sun with its movement produce frequencies that are too slow to be registered by human ears, but, as Rupert Sheldrake reminds us, "if there were a galactic mind, then it might well hear…a kind of planetary, stellar and galactic music." Moreover, the fundamental particles of matter, being patterns of vibration, "are all vibratory structures. Indeed, everything in nature is rhythmic or vibratory, including our own physiology," and thus music is everywhere. It follows that "Music can link us to musical minds far greater than our own, and ultimately to the source of life itself."

43.

God Is an Infinite Voice

JOHN OF THE CROSS SAYS "God is an infinite voice [who] produces the effect of an immense voice." In this passage, John is discussing the sacred sounds that "resounding rivers" make, sounds that "are so loud that they muffle and suppress every other sound." He is talking about the bounty and brilliance of nature and how being present to it can wash away the busy sounds of human interaction and bustle that can shut our souls down. In God there is a "delightful experience,…this divine onslaught God causes in the soul is like a resounding river which fills everything with peace and glory." Such a beautiful sound takes over the soul, which becomes "possessed by it, for it seems to be not merely the sound of rivers but the sound of roaring thunder."

This teaching seems echoed 300 years earlier by Meister Eckhart when he said each creature is "gladly doing the best it can to express Divinity." The idea of God as Word or *Dabhar* is being celebrated here. God speaks to us through creatures. As John of the Cross puts it, "Each of them is endowed with a certain likeness of God and in its own way gives voice to what God is in it." Indeed, creatures become for the soul "a harmonious symphony of sublime music surpassing all concerts and melodies of the world," for "all creatures raise their voice in testimony to what God is."

44.

God Is Logos or Word

"In the beginning was the Word and the Word was with God and the Word was God." So begins the Gospel of John. (1.1) For pre-modern peoples, before the invention of the printing press, every creature was considered a "word of God"—not just words on a printed page of a Bible. Eckhart says that "every creature is a word of God" and "is full of God and is a book" about God and Aquinas declared that "visible creatures are like a book in which we read the knowledge of God. One has every right to call God's creatures God's 'words,' for they express the divine mind just as effects manifest their cause. 'The Works of the Lord are the words of the Lord' (Eccles. 42.15)."

I have long felt that the word "Dabhar" (in Greek, *Logos*) that we translate as "Word" can be easily distorted in a wordy and anthropocentric society like ours has become. Indeed, I translated "Dabhar" as "energy" in my book *Original Blessing* written over thirty-five years ago. Hildegard of Bingen captured the dynamism inherent in a creature that is a living word of God when she writes: "God's Word is in all creation, visible and invisible. The Word is living, being, spirit, all verdant greening, all creativity. All creation is awakened, called, by the resounding melody, God's invocation of the Word. This Word manifest in every creature. Now this is how the spirit is in the flesh—the Word is indivisible from God." This "Word of God" theology is also found in the Cosmic Christ, Buddha Nature and Image of God theology. (See #73) The "*Logos*" or Word is the Cosmic Christ present in every creature.

45.

God Is Wisdom

NICHOLAS OF CUSA SAYS that "the *Logos* of creation in whom all things were created can be nothing other than divine wisdom." He warns us that Wisdom is not found so much in human books as in the human heart and in all of creation. In the Bible, Wisdom (in Greek, *Sophia*; in Hebrew, *Hokhmah*) is pictured as cosmic and feminine. "My dwelling place was in high heaven, my throne was in a pillar of cloud. Alone I made a circuit of the sky and traversed the depth of the abyss." (Sirach 24:5-6) We are told Wisdom is a "friend of the prophets" (Wisdom 7:27) and that "whoever loves her loves life." (Sirach 4:12) She was present at the origin of the world, "from the beginning, before earth came into being. The deep was not, when I was born, there were no springs to gush with water. Before the mountains were settled, before the hills, I came to birth." She was busy at delight and play "everywhere in the world." (Proverbs 8:23-25, 31)

Aquinas teaches that "God is the origin of Wisdom" and is known through visible creatures we read like we do the book of nature. Kabbalist teaching tells us that the key to learning the wondrous paths of Wisdom is sucking. "This is meditation through sucking, not through knowing." Hildegard of Bingen celebrates Wisdom's presence throughout nature:

> I, the fiery life of divine wisdom,
> I ignite the beauty of the plains,
> I sparkle the waters,
> I burn in the sun, and the moon, and the stars.
> With wisdom I order all rightly.
> Above all I determine truth.

46.

God Is the Tao

IN CHINA THE TAO is honored as "the Great Mother, Mother of the universe" who is "always present within you." She is both cosmic and intimate. She "flows through all things, inside and outside and returns to the origin of all things." All things obey her for while humans follow the earth and the earth follows the universe, "the universe follows the Tao. The Tao follows only itself." She is the source of all and consequently "every being in the universe is an expression of the Tao" and "every being spontaneously honors the Tao." It is the Tao that "gives birth to all beings, nourishes them, maintains them, cares for them, comforts them, protects them." And "that is why love of the Tao is in the very nature of things."

47.

God Is a Circle

HILDEGARD OF BINGEN had a vision in which "a wheel was shone to me, wonderful to behold...Divinity is in its omniscience and omnipotence like a wheel, a circle, a whole, that can neither be understood, nor divided, nor begun nor ended." Such an image takes us beyond Divinity as a person or projection of a person, where we can see the world and God's place in it in a new perspective.

How else is God like a circle? Eckhart says that "being is a circle for God" and Black Elk talks about how all things in nature are *round*, a bird's nest, the seasons, the sun, moon, stars, earth, even our being born, living, and dying. There is a "sacred hoop" within which we all live and move and have our being. Aquinas says that "Love works in a circle" between lover and beloved and creatures reveal "a kind of circular motion" emerging "from their first Source" and returning to it at the end.

It would seem that Creation and Creator are biased in favor of circles and of spirals which are open-ended circles in motion. The four paths of creation spirituality are also best envisioned as spirals or expanding and open-ended circles and certainly not as steps up a ladder.

48.

God Is a Source
without a Source

WE ALL SEEK TO KNOW the sources of things, to arrive at the source, to follow a river or a creek to its origins, indeed to know our own origins. And we seek to know the source of all things, the source of the universe. Aquinas calls God "A source without a source." God is a being with no source, a Sourceless Being, the Divine source is built into Divinity itself. It is subject to nothing, to no other source. Hart calls God "the unconditioned source of all things." Eckhart talks of our dying as a "return to our source," a return to the Godhead where unity is total.

A great mystery, this, that Rumi also sings about:

Everything you see has its roots
    In the Unseen world.
The forms may change,
    yet the essence remains the same.

Every wondrous sight will vanish,
Every sweet word will fade.
　　　　But do not be disheartened,
The Source they came from is eternal—
Growing, branching out,
giving new life and new joy....
The Source is full,
Its waters are ever-flowing:
　　　　Do not grieve,
　　　　drink your fill!
Don't think it will ever run dry—
This is the endless Ocean!

Aquinas observes that there are two kinds of water—living water and stagnant water. What is the difference? Living waters are connected to their source, he reminds us.

49.

God Is Mother

THE ANCIENT *VEDAS* OF INDIA call God "motherliest" and the fourteenth century English mystic Julian of Norwich developed the Motherhood of God in a profound way. She writes: "God feels great delight to be our Mother.... The deep Wisdom of the Trinity is our Mother. In her we are all enclosed...." Indeed, God is "our true mother in whom we are endlessly carried and out of whom we will never come." Again, "Just as God is truly our Father, so also is God truly our Mother....God is the true Father and Mother of Nature."

Ramakrishna teaches this about the Divine Mother: "Whatever we see or think about is the manifestation of the Mother, of the Primordial Energy, the Primal Consciousness....The Primordial Power is "ever at play." She is creating, preserving, and destroying in play, as it were. He advises us to "Pray to the Divine Mother with a longing heart. Her vision dries up all craving...and completely destroys all attachment."

The *Tao Te Ching* calls the Tao the "Great Mother of the Universe."

50.

God Is Father, Abba

THE FAVORITE NAME for God invoked by the historical Jesus is "Abba" or Father or Papa. The *Vedas* call God "most fatherly of fathers." A father protects and directs, offers pathways and teaches the ways of the world to his offspring. "Father Sky" is an ancient archetype for the powers of the heavens and for the inherently beautiful sense of the sacred masculine that is found in about 90% of human cultures the world over.

51.

God Is Godhead

MEISTER ECKHART DISTINGUISHES "God" from "Godhead" and says they are as different and far apart as the earth from the heavens. In his two languages God is masculine (*"Gott"* in German; *"Deus"* in Latin) and Godhead is feminine ("Gottheit" in German and "Deitas" in Latin). God is about *action*—Creator, Liberator, Redeemer, History and the rest; but the Godhead is about *mystery* more than history; about being more than doing; about silence more than action. We dwell first in the Godhead and we return to the Godhead when we die. In between, at birth, we enter the world of God and creation.

52.

God Is the Final Cause
of All Creation

HART EMPHASIZES THAT GOD is not only the source of all being and consciousness but also "the final cause of all creation, the end toward which all beings are moved, the power of infinite being that summons all things into existence from nothingness and into union with itself." We receive glimpses of this union in our epiphanies and experiences of ecstasy, which constitute the "breakthroughs" we undergo in this life of a temporary revelation or lifting of the veil between ourselves and the Godhead. As Meister Eckhart put it, "in breakthrough I learn that God and I are one." Thus, for Hart, "God is thus experienced as that bliss in which our natures have their consummation." Says Eckhart: "Within its very self nature seeks and strives for God."

Aquinas teaches that "all things desire God as their end whenever they desire any good whatsoever." And Howard Thurman recognizes God as "the goal of man's life, the end of all his seeking, the meaning of all his striving. God is the guarantor of all his values, the ultimate meaning—the timeless frame of reference."

53.

God Is Our Aspirations

NANCY ABRAMS SAYS HUMANS "are the aspiring species." In many ways to talk of aspirations is to talk about final cause for a species like ours that makes choices. Abrams proposes "Aspiration" as her sole name for God: *"God is endlessly emerging from the staggering complexity of all humanity's aspirations across time."* She elaborates.

> Aspirations must be real, because they are our defining characteristics; they are our purpose. They play out in our behavior and beliefs and interactions with each other....Aspirations are the stories of our future, the stories we live for. Aspirations are among the abstractions, like love, that are the most real to us.
>
> The idea that God is a phenomenon that emerges from human aspirations turns out to be astonishingly fertile....This ever-emerging God can be understood as the dynamic presence

of what humanity has *collectively* achieved. In this sense God is indeed a creator—of toolmaking, ritual, and language and later of ideals like truth, freedom, and equality, which have taken hundreds of generations to clarify in practice.

Abrams recognizes this God in her study of science.

> The emerging God also can be seen as the guiding force of science. If every astronomer, for example, had to start over observing the stars, no one would ever understand anything. Thousands of years of humans aspiring to understand the heavens better, and aspiring to build on each other's work, were necessary to arrive at the science we have today.….The emerging God has developed meaningful concepts of love and beauty, as well as power and greed.…This emergent phenomenon is worthy of the name God. And it may be the only thing that exists in the modern universe that is…. *Each of us is directly connected to the emerging God.* We can draw on God's power by identifying with the ancient and uplifting force of aspiration that is in us as members of the human species.

54.

God Is the Beyond

OTTO RANK, A PSYCHOLOGICAL genius and, in my opinion, a spiritual genius as well, recognized that "the individual is not just striving for survival but is reaching for some kind of 'beyond.'" He says "we negotiate with the problem of the Beyond" when we approach art and love. We taste these "Beyond" experiences in love and truth and art and they serve to dissolve our individuality and connect us to a "greater whole." This greater whole is the "*unio mystica*," the mystical union, where we experience a "potential restoration of a union with the Cosmos, which once existed and was then lost."

To speak of the "Beyond" is to speak of something that is not yet reached, something that beckons us, reaches out to us. The word in English comes from *being yonder*, being someplace we are not yet, at a frontier, an edge, an adventure, a horizon. We are invited to render the Beyond present, to bring the future into the Now. Is God and a promised Kingdom of God of peace and justice (see #80) such an horizon, a kind of goal, a distant one we long for and strive to create? The theological word for the beyond is *eschaton*.

55.

God Is "Emmanuel,"
God-With-Us

BIBLICAL SCHOLAR HELEN KENIK teaches that "Emmanuel" (God-with-us) is in fact the most ancient name for Divinity in the Bible. To say that God is "God-With-Us" is to deconstruct the hierarchical notion that God is above us looking down on us and judging us. This has profound ramifications as Dorothee Soelle points out when she writes: "In feminist theology therefore, the issue is not about exchanging pronouns, but about another way of thinking of transcendence. Transcendence is no longer to be understood as being independent of everything and ruling over everything else, but rather as *being bound up in the web of life*....That means that we move from God-above-us to God-within-us and overcome false transcendence hierarchically conceived."

56.

God Is the Web of Life

AN AFFIRMATION OF THE WEB of life and acknowledgement of interdependence is at stake when we conceive transcendence not as "upness" and ladder climbing to get to the top but as a web of life, a dancing of Sara's Circle rather than a climbing of Jacob's ladder. A Divinity among us, not over us. And the "us" is all beings interdependent as we are. All creation. All our relations. Community is another name for a web of life, each part contributing to the whole.

57.

God Is the "One Face" that Is Expressed in All the Other Faces in Creation

ACCORDING TO FIFTEENTH CENTURY scientist and mystic Nicolas of Cusa, every creature is a face of the One Face who is God. "In all faces is seen the Face of faces, veiled in a billion riddles...." The Quran teaches: "To God belongs the East and the West; in whatever direction you turn to look, there is the Face of God." (2:115).

58.

God Is the Wounds of the Universe and the Wounding in Human Lives as Well

BUDDHISM SPEAKS BLUNTLY about the "suffering of all beings" and how this is part of Reality as we know it. Christianity also presents, in its images of the suffering and crucified Christ, an archetype of woundedness and suffering in all beings including the innocent and just. The lesson taught is that even God suffers. This Rabbi Heschel insisted on as well, what he called the "pathos" and vulnerability of Divinity. God is not an unmoved mover but an eminently vulnerable Being who undergoes Divine Pathos and suffering with the rest of creation. "God's participation in human history...finds its deepest expression in the fact that God can actually suffer."

59.

God Is the Goddess

GOD IS ALSO KNOWN AS THE GODDESS. The Divine Feminine is an important name for the Deity that often gets forgotten when Patriarchy rules unchecked. Marija Gimbutas, a very accomplished anthropologist who spent her life finding and uncovering myriad artifacts and relics from the goddess times has this to say about the Goddess: "The Goddess in all her manifestations was a symbol of the unity of all life in Nature. Her power was in water and stone, in tomb and cave, in animals and birds, snakes and fish, hills, trees, and flowers. Hence the holistic and mythopoeic perception of the sacredness and mystery of all there is on Earth."

The Goddess has many names. While we are free to apply every name we have given to "God" to the "Goddess," some unique names have been forged for the goddess as well. (Among them are numbers 60-70.)

60.

God Is Tara

THE NAME "TARA" is a Tibetan name that means both "Star" and "Tear." Mahayana Buddhism worships the Divine Mother as Tara, who is said to have been born out of one of the tears of the Buddha of compassion that fell to the earth. She who saves and restores was born from that tear. She offers liberation and illumination in our everyday life. Enlightenment is available to all. She is addressed in a Tibetan litany as "Our mother: great compassion! Our mother: a thousand hands, a thousand eyes!; Our mother: Cooling like water!; Our mother: ripening like fire!; our mother: spreading like wind!; Our mother: pervading like space!"

61.

God Is Kuan Yin

IN CHINA, KUAN YIN is considered the Bodhisattva of Compassion who listens and responds to the cries of all beings. Like Mary and Artemis, she is a virgin Goddess who "protects women, offers them a religious life as an alternative to marriage, and grants children to those who want them." She is omnipresent for "in the lands of the universe there is no place where she does not manifest herself" and her wondrous compassion everywhere "pours spiritual rain like nectar" everywhere while "quenching the flames of distress."

63.

God Is Isis

Isis is the primordial Great Goddess in Egypt, the African mother of deities, the sun and the world itself. Her name means "throne" and the pharaohs of old, both male and female, claimed their lineage from her. She guaranteed the fertility of the land and guarded over the dead. In an ancient prayer she declares: "I am Nature, the universal Mother, Mistress of all the elements, primordial child of time, sovereign of all things spiritual,… the single manifestation of all gods and goddesses that are…." The tears of Isis are said to have launched the Nile river. She was a miracle worker and healer and her son, Osiris, was resurrected from the dead.

Erich Neumann exegetes the deeper meanings behind Isis as Throne when he writes: "As mother and earth woman, the Great Mother is the 'throne' pure and simple….To be taken on the lap, is like being taken to the breast, a symbolic expression for adoption of the child, and also of the man, by the Feminine."

64.

God Is the Black Madonna

THE BLACK MADONNA, commemorated in shrines in Sicily, Russia, Poland, Czechoslovakia, France, Spain, Switzerland, Germany, derives from the African goddess Isis whose name as we just saw means "throne." The great 12th century renaissance was in great part inspired by a return of the Goddess and included the birth of a new exciting architecture found in the Gothic Cathedral movement. This, the Gothic revolution, as Henry Adams convincingly argued in his classic work, *Mount Saint Michel and Chartres*, was a direct assault on the Romanesque and singularly masculine symbolism of the dark ages. The very word "cathedra" means *throne*—a Cathedral is where the goddess sits ruling over the city with love and justice, celebration and compassion. It is no coincidence that in many of these medieval gothic cathedrals there sits a Black Madonna mirrored after the goddess Isis.

The Black Madonna stood for many things including, according to China Galand, "life, life with all its teeming diversity of peoples, our different colors, our fullness." She also represented grief, celebration, the cosmos, people of color, and much more.

65.

God Is Kali

KALI IS THE BLACK MADONNA of the East who represents chaos and destruction that can lead to new life.
Andrew Harvey and Carolyn Baker believe that she is
an archetype for our turbulent times for she demands
strength and rootedness to see us through this collective
dark night that our globe finds itself in today.

66.

God Is Mary

HILDEGARD OF BINGEN CALLS MARY "ground of all being" and prays to her this way: "In you, mild virgin, is the fullness of all joy." To Hildegard Mary is a "luminous mother, holy, healing art" who has "conquered death" and "established life." She prays to her: "Ask for us life. Ask for us radiant joy. Ask for us the sweet, delicious ecstasy that is forever yours." Mary is the "Mother of all joy" and a "glowing, most green, verdant sprout" who "buds forth into light."

All the gothic cathedrals were inspired by Mary, and hundreds were named after her, "Notre Dame de Paris, Notre Dame de Chartres, Notre Dame de Lyon," etc. Why was she such an inspiration to the medieval renaissance? Cultural historian Henry Adams felt it was because she represented the imperfection of human love. She represented a refuge for "whatever was irregular, exceptional, outlawed; and this was the whole human race." It was her humanity that stood out and her care for wounded humanity. She represented "a Unity that brought together Duality, Diversity, Infinity and Sex!" She came along when the University was invented in the West, "the Virgin of the twelfth and thirteenth centuries had not only the powers of Eve and Demeter and Venus; she was also the mistress of all the arts and sciences, was afraid of none of them and did nothing, ever, to stunt any of them."

Mary was understood as being "above law" and represented "the whole rebellion of man against fate; the whole protest against divine law." She was not about saving soul or body as much as a symbol of "sympathy with people who suffered under law—justly or unjustly, by accident or design, by decree of God or by guile of Devil." Her essence was "positive compassion; she was what might be called the Buddhist element in Christianity, for with her as with Buddha compassion is [primary]. To Kwannon the Compassionate One and to Mary the Mother of God, compassion included the idea of sorrowful contemplation."

67.

God Is Our Lady of Guadalupe
The Brown Madonna

SHORTLY AFTER SPANISH INVADERS took over much of Mexico, a young Indian named Juan Diego visited a Hill where the Goddess of Earth and Corn had enjoyed a major temple in her honor for centuries. There the Lady of Guadalupe appeared to him as a pregnant, dark-skinned Indian woman clothed with stars and moon and rays of the sun. She spoke to Juan in his indigenous language and has come to symbolize freedom from invaders and colonizers. A symbol of resistance, she was "a warrior goddess who blessed the cultural and political weapons of activists and artists," writes one commentator. "She was against racism, the border patrol cops, and supremacist politicians." And she stood with other strong women such as Frida and Sor Juana on behalf of women's rights.

68.

God Is Shekinah

THIS WORD, WHICH IS FEMININE IN HEBREW, speaks to a special "presence" of God or a divine manifestation where the Divine is felt to be present. It derives from the word "dwelling," or the verb "to dwell" and speaks to a special dwelling place that occurs among us. God's presence is named by it, God's "amongness" is named. God among us. It can stand for another name for God therefore.

69.

God Is Gaia
Mother Earth

IF EVERY BEING CAN be another name for God, as Aquinas taught, then surely Earth, our Mother in so many ways, our home so blessed and so richly endowed with beauty and life and diverse and wonderful creatures, can be another name for God. Hildegard sings thus:

> The earth is at the same time mother,
> She is mother of all that is natural,
> mother of all that is human.
> She is the mother of all,
> for contained in her are the seeds of all....

70.

God Is Chaos

IN THE GODDESS TIMES, Chaos was honored as a goddess and was consciously (and unconsciously) included into the culture. But when patriarchy took over, the stories changed dramatically and the goddess Chaos became an enemy needing to be slain by masculine warriors. For example, in the Babylonian creation myth, the *Enuma Elish*, the story is told of how the goddess Tiamat is slain by a new god named Marduk. Marduk cuts open the belly of Tiamat in a very vicious murder scene. Marduk was celebrated as a hero and rituals were held annually to celebrate his murder of the goddess. Parallel stories circulated in Greece where Apollo slays a female goddess who guards the shrine of Mother Earth and is considered the source of evil.

This same spirit of Chaos as the enemy—"kill the goddess"—is alive and well today in all acts of misogyny including religious fundamentalism and political fascism. These two movements, that so often go to bed together, insist that law and order take precedence over love, justice and compassion. Both are rigorously anti-women and misogynistic. Both bolster Patriarchy and yearn for a nostalgic past when, supposedly, the masculine ruled over creativity and kept all things in order.

Scientist Ralph Abraham, in his brilliant book, *Chaos, Gaia, Eros*, argues very convincingly that patriarchal religion—and beginning with 18th century modern science—carried on this antipathy toward the feminine and the goddess in the name of order and heresy-hunting which is based on a deep fear of chaos on the part of the masculine psyche. But with the discovery (better, re-discovery) of the positive role of chaos by scientific chaos theory beginning in the 1960's (and Abraham was one of the founders of chaos theory), Chaos was no longer seen as an existential threat. Within weather systems, ellipses of planets, within nature as a whole, chaos was an integral and necessary part of the creativity and unfolding of nature everywhere. Chaos seems part of all creative processes. She has returned as a goddess.

We need to dance a new but ancient dance that incorporates both order and chaos, respecting the power of each. With climate change and much else happening, we should all prepare ourselves for entertaining more chaos, not less.

71.

God Is the Trinity

WHILE ACKNOWLEDGING THE ONENESS of God and God as oneness there are also teachings that God is Triune, that is that there are faces or energies to God that are distinct yet unified. This teaching is found among ancient Celtic peoples and people of India and also in the Triune Divinity of Christianity named as "Father, Son and Spirit" or Father-Mother Creator God and Liberating, Redeeming Son and Breath-bestowing Holy Spirit. Human insistence on the Unity of God is not the last word about God. There is diversity and there is community within the Godhead. The Trinity in Christian teaching is a kind of celebration of diversity even within the Godhead, a sort of warning not to take the Unity of Divinity too literally, that even Divinity has varied personalities and energies and interacts as a community.

The archetype of a Trinitarian Deity is found in many parts of the world. New Grange, the ancient shrine in Ireland, which dates to about 4000 BC, is so designed that the sun shines down its shaft on December 21, the winter solstice. At its entrance there is a giant rock and on the rock are carved three large Spirals. What do these represent? One scholar describes the following three categories as being integral to the triune work of the Goddess: 1. Creation. 2. Transformation. 3. Celebration. Creation includes "birth, nurturance, and the abundance of the natural world." Transformation includes physical death and rebirth as well as the metaphorical deaths and rebirths of trance and descent to the underworld. Celebration encompasses "sexuality, sensuality and creativity. The unity of birth, growth, death and rebirth is the basis of the Goddess's teachings. We see them daily in the cycles of night and day, waking and sleeping, creating and letting go."

Hart builds his search for definitions of God today around a trinity of Being, Consciousness and Bliss, which corresponds to a Hindu Trinity of *Sat, Chit,* and *Ananda.* "God is the one act of being, consciousness, and bliss in whom everything lives and moves and has its being" and God "donates everything that we are to us out of his infinite plenitude of being, consciousness, and bliss."

Poet Emily Dickinson, who was also a serious botanist and gardener, had her own version of a Trinity to which she prayed and it differs from the orthodoxies of a more anthropocentric religion.

> In the name of the Bee—
> And of the Butterfly—
> And of the Breeze—Amen

This is not a theologically simplistic prayer—there is something deep and sophisticated at work here. She is supplanting an anthropocentric and person-centered Trinity with a creation-centered one. After all, the Bee keeps creation going by pollinating flowers and grasses; the Butterfly undergoes a life, death and resurrection cycle comparable to the Paschal mystery of Christ as it evolves and even dies in its evolution from caterpillar to beautiful (but short-lived) winged creature; and the Breeze is wind, Spirit, breath ("spirit" and "wind" or "breeze" are the same words in the Biblical languages and many languages around the world and the Spirit came at Pentecost in the form of wind). The impact of her Trinity is especially poignant because the argument of a Trinitarian vs Unitarian Godhead was a hot one in New England in her day. The Unitarian church was born of that debate after all. She is stepping into the patriarchal debate around the Trinity with all-new—and far more ancient and shamanistic—imagery. But Dickinson sidesteps the theological niceties entirely by simply creating her own Trinity, one based on a more-than-human creation, and challenges both arguing parties with new language and fresh insight born of her medicine womanhood.

72.

God Is The Holy One

RABBI HESCHEL DECLARES THAT "the word holiness is the most precious word in religion." This word, *qadosh*, holy, "more than any other is representative of the mystery and majesty of the divine." Yet what is holiness? Mystic and praise poet Mary Oliver in her poem, "At the River Clarion," which explores who God is, sings about how every creature—the river, the stone in the river, the moss in the river, we humans too, are all "part of holiness." Yes, we creatures are all *parts of holiness* and that is why we are, each of us, worthy names for "God." But only God is "The Holy One." We creatures are *multiple holy ones.* And we humans (unlike the other creatures) often fall short.

73.

God Is The Cosmic Christ
or Buddha Nature; or Image of God

ANOTHER NAME FOR THE HOLY ONE as found within every creature is the Cosmic Christ (a Christian term); or the Buddha Nature (a Buddhist term); or the Image of God (a Jewish term). All point to the Divinity within all things, the "light within all things." The Catholic monk Thomas Merton says "the Blinding One speaks to us gently in ten thousand things....He shines not on them but from within them." But this same light also exists within the one big thing: The universe itself. As Paul put it, "Christ is the one who holds all things in unity... everything in the heavens and everything on the earth." (Col. 1.15-20) Little did he know that "the heavens" were two trillion galaxies large! But now we do know that. So our modest inkling of the Cosmic Christ has grown vastly in our lifetimes. Another name for the Cosmic Christ is Cosmic Wisdom.

74.

God Is the Ultimate "I am" and the "I am" in Everything

When Moses asks God, "Whom shall I tell the people sent me?" God responds: "Tell them that 'I am' sent you." (This can also be translated as "I am who I will be.") The God-name as "I am" is repeated often in the Christian Gospels, especially that of John where the Christ is reported to say "I am the Good Shepherd," "I am the door," "I am the Living Light," "I am the Resurrection", etc. Every being has its own "I am" and this corresponds to the Ground of Being, the Divine presence in all things. In the Gospel of Thomas we read: "Split the wood and I am there; Lift the stone and I am there."

Hart connects the "I am" name of God to the necessity of God, the source of all. He says the designation "I am that I am" is a "proper name" for God for only God is necessary in the universe. Everything else is contingent—even if there were multiple universes, only God is the necessary one.

75.

God Is a Lion and Destroyer of Darkness and Evil

THE VEDAS REFER TO GOD as the "Destroyer of Darkness and Evil." The prophets of Israel speak on behalf of the God of justice who struggles against injustice, lies and denial, war and envy, despair and fear, avarice and hatred. This struggle is part of the work of the God of Justice and the God of Compassion. They require warrior energy to see us through. That is why the Lion, the "king of beasts," is often a symbol for the Divine especially in a desert area where the Bible stories emerged, an area where in ancient times lions inhabited the desert wilderness of what is today Israel. Hildegard of Bingen calls for warrior energy to take on the "adversary" and she equates lion energy with a strong will.

Acting to "destroy darkness" is not about demonizing darkness (we will see in Part II that a valid name for the Divine is *Darkness*), but the darkness referred to here is *moral* darkness. God sustains those who persevere in the struggle against such darkness and evil in themselves and in society. While the lion symbolizes solar light and virility, the wild lioness is a symbol of the Magna Mater, the Great Mother who also cares passionately about justice and defending her oppressed children.

Scientist Arne Wyller emphasizes how young the human mind is and what a tenuous hold it has in linking to the Mind Field. Humans alone among creatures indulge in evil and "it may be the greatest evolutionary gamble the Mind Field has ever taken to imbed some of its own mind quality into the as yet imperfect and unfinished human brain." The Mind Field is restricted to intervene directly in individual human suffering but what follows from this is in fact "an increased human responsibility to participate in the evolutionary experiment of which we are part and parcel. *We humans share with the Mind Field a responsibility to alleviate human suffering and gradually extinguish the human element of evil.*" Wyller believes that there is a biological aspect of evil in human behavior that derives from "the imperfect coupling between the rational part of the human brain and the emotive and reptilian parts.....The evilness may be triggered by the reptilian part, which generates aggression and the sense of self-survival." He invokes Dietrich Bonhoeffer who said that humans must act "as if God did not exist." He writes: "The idea that humans create evil by their imperfect mastery of the evolutionary gifts of the Mind Field, the rational brains, the emotive brain, and the reptilian brain, one on top of the other, in no way needs to reflect on the attributes of the Mind Field."

76.

God Is the True Rest

JULIAN OF NORWICH CALLS GOD "the True Rest" who wants to be known and who finds pleasure in being "our true resting place." This teaching echoes that of Meister Eckhart who talks of how all creatures seek "repose" and how "God enjoys the divine nature which is repose." All creatures are born of repose, it is our origin. God seeks love in creatures but also repose in them.

How is this done? By offering a "quiet heart" says Eckhart. "Nothing resembles God so much as repose," he insists. This repose can happen in the midst of activity and is part and parcel of our creativity and co-creation with God.

77.

God Is a Great Bird

THE BIRD SOARS ON HIGH, IT HAS PERSPECTIVE, it sees
for great distances (a hawk, we are told can see its prey
from two miles away). The Holy Spirit is sometimes
pictured as a bird and Great Birds are often honored for
their spiritual powers, perhaps because they soar above
the Earth where God also dwells. Among these great and
honored birds are the Great Eagle (North America); the
Condor (South America); and the Wild Goose (Siberia
and Celtic countries). In shamanistic traditions very
often there is a reference to a "magic flight" undertaken
with a large winged bird bringing a message to tell the
people. Hildegard wrote a poem and song about the
"moving force of Wisdom" encompassing all in a great
circle and flying on three vast wings.

A Sufi scholar teaches that the Great Bird represents
"the transcendent nature of God, the One who can fly
anywhere." Rumi, addressing his master, prays:

> "You are the great bird of Mount Sinai—
> O master, don't drop me from your beak!"

78.

God Is the Wilderness and Destroyer

I HAVE A FRIEND who talks about the wilderness as his religion and his church. He received a great healing there as a teenager when going through a major grief event caused by the divorce of his parents. As an adult he retreats often to undergo vision quests and to lead others in the wilderness. Eckhart often speaks of God as the "wilderness" and the "desert." There is a wildness to divinity that can otherwise be tamed in our too anthropocentric worlds.

The prophet Hosea talks about "luring Israel out into the wilderness and there speaking to her heart to heart." (Hos 2.16, 14) And Jesus on numerous occasions withdrew into the desert to pray. As recorded in Mark's gospel, following his baptism Jesus was "driven by the Spirit" into the wilderness for forty days where he encountered, among other things, wild beasts, angels, and temptations from the devil. (Mk 1.12-13)

Eckhart recognizes the wilderness as a special encounter with the Divine as well when he says: "There is no room for two in the desert. There Creator and creature are one." Of course the wilderness in the Biblical land of Israel is the desert. "We dwell in unity and in the desert [and] hear the eternal Word.... God in his wilderness and in his own ground." Furthermore, "God leads this spirit into the desert and solitude of himself where he is pure unity and gushes up only within himself." Buddhist poet Gary Snyder equates the sacred with the wild and of course the wilderness is not just the mountains and forests and desert but also *the ocean*. The ocean, our mother, is wilderness also.

Part of wilderness is danger (and possible destruction). Speaking of God as Wilderness therefore is also speaking of *God as Destroyer*. To leave that element out of our grasp of the Godhead is to invite sentimentalism as Father Bede Griffith warns us when he reminds us that "every serious religious tradition admits of this 'terrible' aspect of the Godhead." Jesus after all speaks not only of his yoke being light but also he curses people and talks of bringing a sword and separating households.

79.

God Is the Transcendent Care of All Creatures, Especially Endangered Ones

IF ST JOHN OF THE CROSS can talk of his Beloved as the mountains and the valleys and the islands; and if St Thomas Aquinas can talk of God (citing the Scriptures) as the sun, stone, dew, cloud, air, water, fire, rock, then surely we can name our choices of God-like creatures found in creation. Let me propose a very finite list: God is…rainforests, oceans, elephants, polar bears, gazelles, grizzly bears, lions, tigers, fishes, soil, trees, plants, etc. And all other beings that are beautiful faces of the Divine but are endangered and in peril in our time. It is here that Rabbi Heschel's naming of God as "the transcendent care for being" speaks profoundly to us today.

Joanna Macy and John Seed have created a ritual to name and remember and stand up on behalf of the dying ones in our midst called the "Council of All Beings." This is an honorable and empowering ceremony to undergo.

It is a remembrance of the killing of the Buddha Nature, the Cosmic Christ, the Image of God in beautiful earth creatures occurring in our time and on our watch. Ecocide is real and it is happening in real time.

80.

God Is the Kingdom of God

IN MANY RESPECTS the historical Jesus chose to talk more about *Where God is to be found* than *Who* God is. In doing so, he invoked the term "kingdom of God" or "realm of God" or "reign of God" or "kingdom/queendom of God" at the very heart of his teaching. His listeners understood this "kingdom" very much in contrast to that of the Roman Empire under which they were chafing.

New Testament scholar Bruce Chilton understands the concept this way: "The promise of God's kingdom is that people will finally come to realize divine justice and peace in all that they do....The Kingdom is a matter of both perceiving God's will and doing God's will—on earth as it is in heaven." This means that "human greed and tyranny" are removed and replaced by "a common passion for divine justice." In such a kingdom the homeless are housed, the hungry eat, the sick are cared for. The promise is that the God of justice and compassion will displace false gods of power and might.

Biblical scholar Krister Stendahl says that every time we see the word *basileia*, which we translate as "kingdom," we have a right to translate it as *creation*. Thus the whole universe with all its holy beings constitutes the Kingdom of God; it is already "in our midst." (Luke 17:21)

PART II

Names for the God Without a Name
The Apophatic Divinity

WE HAVE CONSIDERED IN PART I 80 out of trillions of possible names for the Divine based on how every creature qualifies for such a naming. However Aquinas alerts us to the fact that "the Divine One is none of these beings insofar as God surpasses all things." Eckhart says: "No one can really say what God is. The ineffable one has no name." Mystical traditions East and West agree on this truth and how our feeble language cannot hold the Divine Name as we shall see below.

Another way to consider the apophatic Divinity is to consider how every name we offered in Part I is a metaphor. Metaphors are wonderful—and they are necessary for lively discourse about what matters. All the great experiences of life, when we try to name them, are essentially metaphors including Love, Death, Sex, Spirit, God, etc. Metaphors say a lot but they also leave a lot out, a lot remains unsaid. This is one reason we turn to music and dance and painting and sculpture to express what is beyond words and dwells in the depths of silence.

It is also the reason why literalism kills and is so dangerous, especially when it comes to religious issues. One needs a capacity for letting go and not clinging to enter into the deeper mysteries of life. Even poets, who make their living by offering gifts of fresh metaphors, admit their limits, as Adrienne Rich puts it: "Language

82.

God Is Superessential Darkness

DENNIS THE AREOPAGITE SAYS God is "superessential darkness" and a "darkness beyond light." Eckhart repeats this language and says, "the final end is the mystery of the darkness of the eternal Godhead." Not only does this understanding of Divinity honor the dark and honor our unknowing, it also welcomes and makes room for the unspeakable and ineffable and that which is bigger than words. It makes room for silence and nothingness.

We might ask: Are the mysterious Dark Energy and Dark Matter that scientists teach make up 97% of the universe also images of the Dark Divinity? Does the "double dark" theory plus Divinity as superessential darkness offer humankind a new kind of Trinity in our time? One wrapped in darkness?

83.

God Is the Great Mystery

WHAT IS MYSTERY IS VERY shy around words and namings. Mystery does not want to be named. It wishes to remain hidden. The uniqueness of the Divine, the immensity of the Divine, renders it a great mystery that may well be without any name. Here is how Meister Eckhart put it: "The mystery of the darkness of the eternal Godhead is unknown and never was known and never will be known. God dwells therein, unknown to the Godself."

Mystery invites silence. Hart encourages us to "reflect upon the mystery that manifests itself not as a thing among other things, but as the silent event of being itself." Our distance from nature in today's culture often interferes with this silence. "We see the mystery, are addressed by it, given a vocation to raise our thoughts beyond the apparent world to the source of its possibility....but can approach only when we surrender ourselves to it."

84.

God Is the Ineffable One, the One Without a Name Who Will Never Be Given a Name

MEISTER ECKHART SAYS GOD is the "Ineffable One" and the "Unnameable." God is "without a name and is the denial of all names and has never been given a name—a truly hidden God." Such a teaching allows us all to relax and to cease projecting and certainly to cease going to war against one another "in the name" of whatever God we do or do not worship. (Atheists too can get stuck and overly attached to the name "God." Recently I heard this joke: "What I most dislike about atheists is that they are so busy talking about god all the time.")

Who is this, what is this, that is without a name and whom we can never name? This "It" must be quite amazing because we humans are great at naming everything and anything that comes our way—but we need to cease naming and projecting when it comes to Divinity. How eager we are to seize and to hold and to name and to categorize and to box up into concepts and then rules and then doctrines and then dogmas. But Whoa! Stop! This "God" thing does not yield to such human control compulsions. "God" is the one without a name who will never be given a name. Just being. And non-being. And silence. And….

Words fail us in the face of mystery, as Thich Naht Hanh reminds us, "we know the Holy Spirit as energy and not as notions and words." This is why our deepest feelings and experiences turn us to art and music and dance and silence in response to the Ineffable One.

85.

God Is the Unknown One

THOMAS AQUINAS SAID: "The cause at which we wonder is hidden from us... We are united to God as to one Unknown....God alone knows the depths and riches of the Godhead, and divine wisdom alone can declare its secrets." Eckhart says: "Reason can never comprehend God in the ocean of his unfathomableness." Indeed, for Aquinas the mind's "greatest achievement [is] to realize that God is far beyond anything we think. This is the ultimate in human knowledge: to know that we do not know God...By its immensity the divine essence transcends every form attained by the human intellect." Eckhart echoes this teaching when he says: "whatever one says what God is, God is not; God is what one does not say of God, rather than what one says God is."

Psychotherapist and mystic Estelle Frankel agrees. In her important book, *The Wisdom of Not Knowing*, she invites us to "befriend the unknown" and to "trade the certainty of the known for the unknown." As a lifelong student of Jewish mysticism she has come to learn that "being receptive to the unknown, in all its many facets, allows us to become more open, curious, flexible, and expansive in our personal and professional lives. This openness is the key to all learning and creativity. It is the gate that unlocks our wisdom and courage." She cites the *Zohar*: "Thought cannot encompass Your divine essence" and she retranslates it as, "you cannot wrap your mind around God." Wisdom is dialectical and thus "always involves a synergy of knowing and not knowing, discovery and mystery, action and stillness, words and silence."

86.

God Is Nothingness

THOMAS AQUINAS SAYS THAT "God is said to be non-being (*non existens*) not because God is lacking in being but because God is beyond all beings." Meister Eckhart develops this idea when he declares that "God is a being beyond being and a nothingness beyond being" who consists of a "changeless existence and a nameless nothingness." He elaborates on this difficult-to-grasp concept which in fact goes beyond concepts when he says: "God is nothing. It is not, however, as if he were without being. He is rather neither this thing nor that thing that we might express, He is a being above all being. He is a beingless being....God is nothingness, and yet God is something."

Father Bede Griffiths comments on Hindu wisdom regarding God talk: "We cannot name Brahman. It is 'not this, not this.' Whatever word we use, whatever image, whatever concept, we have always to go beyond...One cannot stop with any name of God....We are all seeing that inexpressible mystery beyond, and that is Brahman, which is *neti, neti*, 'not this, not this.'"

In the Kabbalah God is also called Nothingness or *Ayin*, Mystical Nothingness: "*Ayin*, Nothingness, is more existent than all the being of the world…." The Buddhist concept of *Shunyata* or emptiness reminds us that a pregnant emptiness exists within beings and within the context of interconnection. Each being exists only in relationship. Eckhart has a similar teaching when he says "Relation accordingly is present in the essence of a thing, receives its being in the essence…."

87.

God Is the
Annihilation of Thought

JEWISH MYSTICISM CALLS GOD "*Ein Sof*" or "that which thought cannot comprehend." We are reminded that "All is one in the simplicity of absolute undifferentiation. Our limited mind cannot grasp or fathom this, for it joins infinity." In this way we can say that "God is the annihilation of all thoughts, uncontainable by any concept. Indeed, since no one can contain God at all, it is called Nothingness, *Ayin*." If God is the erasure of all thoughts, we can see why meditation as emptying the mind is so fruitful for connecting us to the One. We can see the power of Silence.

Buddhism, in addition to offering multiple meditation practices to empty the mind of thoughts, has lots to say about the nothingness and unknowability of God. Says Thich Nhat Hanh: "It is impossible to use our concepts and words to describe God....It's very wise not to say anything about God. To me the best theologian is the one who never speaks about God." Meister Eckhart is in full agreement when he says: "The most beautiful thing which a person can say about God would be for that person to remain silent from the wisdom of an inner wealth. So, be silent and quit flapping your gums about God."

88.

God Is the Form Without Form

THE *TAO TE CHING* SPEAKS of the Tao as "seamless, unnamable, it returns to the realm of nothing. Form that includes all forms, image without an image, subtle, beyond all conception." God is formless form that embraces all form, an image without image that encircles all images, existing but beyond conceiving, a membrane in which all things live, move and have their being. Eckhart echoes the same teaching when he says "God is a not-God, a not-mind, a not-person, a not-image." Rather God is "a pure, clear One who is separate from all twoness."

89.

God Is Silence

THE PSALMIST ADVISES US TO "Be still and learn that I am God." Meister Eckhart says: "Nothing in all creation is so like God as silence" and he urges us to enter into deep silence to find God. It is best, he says, "to maintain total silence about that which is the source of all things." This is meditation, this is mindfulness. Says Eckhart: "The Word lies hidden in the soul, unknown and unheard unless room is made for it in the ground of hearing, otherwise it is not heard. All voices and sounds must cease and there must be pure stillness within, a still silence." Stillness leads to an encounter with the Divine. Often the encounter is far beyond words.

Says Rumi:

> Secretly we spoke,
> That wise one and me.
> I said, *Tell me the secrets of the world.*
> He said, *Sh…Let silence*
> *Tell you the secrets of the world.*

Hawaiian elder Nana Veary says: "Silence means no repetitions, no affirmations, no denials, only a conscious acknowledgement of God's allness. In the silence, one is beyond words and thoughts."

When brain researcher Andrew Newberg demonstrated that in deep states of meditation we go beyond thought and drop into an "experience of boundlessness," Frankel responded this way: "Evidently, our brains are hardwired to experience the mystical state of oneness we call 'God' and Kabbalists refer to as *ayin* or *Ein Sof* (literally, 'Without End'). Ein Sof is the boundless and transcendent aspect of divinity that is beyond all form....When we emerge from such states of grace, our inner being opens more fully and new layers of soul are revealed to us."

May states of grace be our regular fare and food.

PART III

*Some Practices to Undergo Apropos of the
Names of God Offered in this Book*

Practices for Part I

1. Among the 80 names for God offered here, pick out ten that are most meaningful and useful to you personally at this time in your journey. Reflect on them. Keep a diary about them. Meditate on a different one for a day or for several days at a time.

Ask yourself: How do I experience God this way? Observe how your understanding of Divinity is evolving with these practices. Feel free to journal about your experience.

2. Among the 80 names for God offered here, pick out ten that you feel are most meaningful and useful to culture at large today. Why are they useful at this time in history in your understanding?

Ask yourself: How would culture alter if we were to experience God this way?

3. How do Numbers 1 and 2 above line up for you? Do your personal choices correspond with many of your cultural choices or not? How does one feed the other?

4. Of the 80 names for God offered here, which ones are you least at home with? Why do you suppose this is so? Is it worth diving deeper into those most challenging names? Make a list of them and try meditating on them for a day or several days at a time.

5. Of the 80 names for God offered here, which ones do you think our culture is least at home with? Why do you think that is so? It is worth it to get the culture (and churches and synagogues or mosques) more at home with these names of God? If so, how would you best propose going about that?

6. Of the 80 names for God offered here, which ones surprised you the most? Why do you think that is so?

7. Of the 80 names for God, which ones challenged you the most? What is the reason for that in your opinion?

8. Of the 80 names for God, which ones do you feel you are overly familiar with? Are you bored by them? Is there a way to cure that boredom?

9. Of the 80 names for God, which ones do you feel our culture appears overly familiar with? Why do you think that is so? Is it worth it to try to combat that boredom? If so, how would you suggest going about it?

10. Some blank pages are left after Part I. This is for your adding new and fresh Divine names. Do you have some to add? Write them down. Keep a running list or diary of them.

11. Try ritualizing some of these names for God whether
a. by dancing them;
b. by putting them to music;
c. by playing music that awakens the particular image in you;
d. by rendering them in poetry;
e. by journaling about them;
f. by chanting them mantra-style over and over again;
g. by creating rituals around them.

12. Invite others to ritualize these names for God along with you. Celebrate!

13. Invite others to discuss these names for God with you.

14. Study the "book of nature" by studying science being sure to bring your heart to the study as you would if you were reading and listening to the mystics or to Sacred Scriptures.

15. Study Sacred Scriptures of whatever tradition and listen for the names for God that emerge for you there.

16. Pay attention to these names and images appearing in your dreams.

17. Before going to bed, make a request that a name of God speak to you in your dreams.

Practices for Part II

1.Go into Nature and find beings that speak to you. Be with them in silence, listening deeply.

2. Remember beings in nature that have spoken to you in the past. What have they taught you? What are they eager to teach others through you?

3. Be with the 9 names in Part II in silence, allowing them to speak to you.

4. Have a conversation with others about the 9 names in Part II of this book.

5. Practice a letting go and mind-emptying kind of meditation. Then go back and re-read each of these 9 names for the apophatic Divinity.

6. Which of these 9 names for the Ineffable God speak most deeply to you? Why do you think that is so?

7. Which of these 9 names in Part II are the most challenging for you? What can you learn from this? Why do you think they are problematic for you?

8. What further names for the "unknown" and "unnameable God" come to you in addition to the ones listed in this book? Keep a running list of them. Meditate on them.

9. Practice silence.

10. Practice these names in silence.

11. Practice these names by chanting them mantra-style, over and over.

12. Create personal rituals around one or several of these 9 names in Part II.

13. Create group rituals with others around one or several of these 9 names in Part II.

14. Read reliable mystics like Meister Eckhart and Estelle Frankel on the apophatic Divinity alone or

with others. (See Sermons 11-20 in Fox, *Passion for Creation*, 166-292; and Estelle Frankel, *The Wisdom of Not Knowing*.)

PART IV

Appendix
Aquinas on Names of God

———————

AQUINAS' STATEMENT ON THE MULTIPLE names for God is so startling and so germane to this book that I thought it useful to reproduce the entire section here as an Appendix. I ran across it over twenty years ago when I was translating many of his untranslated works for my book that became *Sheer Joy: Conversations with Thomas Aquinas on Creation Spirituality*. It is found in his very first book, written when he was 28 years old and, as far as I know, had until my study never been translated into either English or Italian or German or French. I believe it deserves our attention today. Commenting on and responding to a passage by the sixth century Syrian monk Dennis the Areopagite's book, *The Divine Names*, Aquinas writes:

> *Even the very ones who were experienced concerning Divinity, such as the apostles and prophets, praise God as the Cause of all things from the many things caused. They praise God as good (Luke 18); as beautiful (Song of Songs 1); as wise (Job 9); as beloved (Song of Songs 5); as God of gods (Ps 50); as holy of holies (Dan. 9); as eternal (Bar. 4); as manifest (Job 14); as the cause of the ages (Eccles. 24); as the bestower of life (Acts 17); as wisdom (1*

Cor. 1); as mind or intellect (Ps. 29); as reason (Is. 63: "I who speak justice"); as the knower (2 Tim. 2); as the one possessing in advance all the treasures of universal knowledge (Col. 2); as virtue (1 Cor. 1); as the powerful (Ps. 89); as King of kings (Apoc. 19); as the Ancient of days (Dan. 7); as without age and unchanging (James 1); as salvation (Matt. 1) ; as justice, or as one justifying, as it were, deliverance or redemption according to another translation (1 Cor. 1); as magnitude exceeding all things (Job 23); as in the light breeze (3 Kings 19).

And they say that God is even in minds or hearts (Eph. 3); in spirits (Wis. 7); and in bodies (1 Cor. 6); in heaven and on earth (Jer. 23); and at the same time in the same place, that is with regard to the same material, they say that the same one is worldly, that is, in the world (John . 1); involved in the world (Eccles. 24); above the world (Is. 66); and supercelestial, or above the heavens (Ps. 113: "The Lord on high above all the nations whose glory is above all the skies"); supersubstantial (Matt. 6); the sun (Mal. 4); a constellation, that is, a star (Apoc. 22); fire (Deut.4); water (John 4); air (Joel 2); and dew (Hos. 14); cloud (Hos. 6); stone (Ps., 118); rock

(1 Cor. 10); and all the other beings attributed to God as cause.

And the Divine One is none of these being insofar as God surpasses all things.

Introduction

"The One Existence the wise call by many names." Rg
Veda in A. C. Bose, *The Call of the Vedas* (Bombay:
Bharatiya Vidya Bhavan, 1988), 30.

"I pray God to rid me of God." Matthew Fox, *Passion
For Creation: The Earth-Honoring Spirituality of
Meister Eckhart* (Rochester, Vt: Inner Traditions,
1991), 217.

"The highest and loftiest thing..." Ibid., 222.

"I think are most beautiful and wonderful and useful for
our times." I cover these and a number of names for
God from various spiritual traditions in my previous
book, *One River, Many Wells: Wisdom Springing from
Global Faiths* (New York: Jeremy P. Tarcher/ Putnam,
2000) chapters 5-9.

"I am indebted and which I have often prayed myself."
Consider, for example, Glenn Pascall, ed.,
*Illumination of the Names: Meditation by Sufi Masters
on the Ninety-Nine Beautiful Names of God* (San
Rafael, CA: International Association of Sufism
Publications, 2011).

"God has a million faces." Swami Prabhavananda and
Christopher Isherwood, trans., *Bhagavad Gita* (New
York: Signet Classics, 2002), 95.

"Even the very ones…" Matthew Fox, *Sheer Joy: Conversations with Thomas Aquinas on Creation Spirituality* (NY: Jeremy P. Tarcher/Putnam, 2003), 182f.

"… in his foundational work, *The Divine Names*." C.D. Rolt, trans., *Dionysius the Areopagite: The Divine Names and the Mystical Theology* (London: SPCK, 1975), 154.

"Philosopher Theodore Richards points out…" Theodore Richards, *The Great Re-imagining: Spirituality in an Age of Apocalypse* (Stonington, CT: Homebound Publications, 2017).

"God becomes where all creatures express God…" Fox, *Passion for Creation*, 78.

"What actually evolved was human understanding…" *Deepak Chopra, God: A Story of Revelation* (NY: HarperOne, 2012), 2f.

"And the Divine One is none of these beings insofar as God surpasses all things." Fox, *Sheer Joy*, 183.

"All creatures want to express God…." Fox, *Passion for Creation*, 62.

"Our thinking about God today…" Nancy Ellen Abrams, *A God That Could Be Real: Spirituality, Science, and The Future of Our Planet* (Boston: Beacon Press, 2015), 146.

"defining the good doesn't necessarily make it happen…"
Ibid., 147.

"Any debate over an intelligent designer…" David Bentley
Hart, *The Experience of God: Being, Consciousness,
Bliss* (New Haven, Ct.: Yale University Press, 2013),
289.

"The reason the very concept of God…." Ibid., 328.

"Perhaps this is attributable…." Ibid., 328f.

"Order of the Sacred Earth." See Matthew Fox, Skylar
Wilson, Jennifer Listug, *Order of the Sacred Earth: An
Intergenerational Vision of Love and Action* (Rhine
beck, NY: Monkfish Book Publishing Company,
2017)

1. God Is Love

"Love is nothing other than God…." Fox, *Passion for
Creation*, 76.

"All the universe is born of Love…" Jonathan Star, trans.,
*A Garden Beyond Paradise: The Mystical Poetry of
Rumi* (NY: Bantam Books, 1992), 113.

"Lose your soul in God's love." Ibid., 93.

"Love causes the earth to tremble." Ibid., 47.

2. God Is Goodness

"I saw that God is everything that is good....everything possesses is God." Brendan Doyle, *Meditations with Julian of Norwich* (Santa Fe, NM: Bear & Co, 1983) 24, 32.

"A good person praises good people." Fox, *Passion for Creation*, 541.

"is sheer goodness ... God is supremely good and therefore supremely generous." Fox, *Sheer Joy*, 96, 99f.

"The good is nothing less than God himself....longing for God." Hart, *The Experience of God*, 254, 275.

3. God Is the One to Whom We Give Our Thanks

"to that original apprehension... comes from beyond all possible beings." Ibid., 150f.

4. God Is Existence, Being and "Isness"

"God is being... fountain of being." Fox, *Passion for Creation*, 72, 539.

"God is pure existence..." Fox, *Sheer Joy*, 87.

"God is not a mythical person..." Deepak Chopra, *The Future of God: A Practical Approach to Spirituality*

For Our Times (New York: Harmony Books, 2014), 253.

"The vast physical mechanism we call the universe…" Ibid., 134.

"all physical reality is contingent." Hart, *The Experience of God*, 145.

"the ultimate source of *existence*." Ibid., 104.

"God's work whereby God… Continually pours out existence into things." Fox, *Sheer Joy,* 125, 126.

"is not an act that happened once upon a time." Abraham Joshua Heschel, *The Sabbath: Its Meaning for Modern Man,* (NY: Noonday Press, 1951), 100.

"may well be the social order." Hart, *The Experience of God*, 331.

"it is far easier to think about beings…we impose upon it." Ibid., 92, 94.

"the giving of being… Isness is God." Fox, *Passion for Creation*, 88f.

"to exist is the most perfect thing of all." Fox, *Sheer Joy*, 81.

5. God Is the Ground of Being

"God's ground is my ground…" Fox, *Passion for Creation,* 472.

"all notions applied…." Thich Nhat Hanh, *Living Buddha, Living Christ* (NY: Riverhead Books, 1995), 188.

"God as the ground of being cannot be conceived of." Ibid., 144.

6. God Is the Cause of Wonder

"immense preciousness of being …is not an object of analysis but a cause of wonder." Abraham Joshua Heschel, *Man Is Not Alone: A Philosophy of Religion* (New York: Farrar, Straus, and Young, 1951), 22.

"Who lit the wonder before our eyes and the wonder of our eyes?" Abraham Joshua Heschel, *God In Search of Man: A Philosophy of Judaism* (NY: Farrar, Straus, and Cudahy, 1955), 106.

"unmitigated wonder… Who could believe it….intrudes first as a sense of wonder." Ibid., 58, 71.

"There is no true science…." William Hermanns, *Einstein and the Poet: In Search of the Cosmic Man* (Brookline Village, Ma: Branden Press Inc., 1983), 108.

"is concerned with the marvelous…. and marvel at divine wisdom." Fox, *Sheer Joy*, 76, 78.

7. God Is the Mind of the Universe

"God is...the mind of the universe... which in this way
comes closer to life." Erich Jantsch, *The Self-Organiz
ing Universe* (NY: Pergamon Press, 1980), 307.
"The divine, however, becomes...." Ibid.

8. God Is Evolution and Pure Potential

"not absolute, he evolves himself....pure potential." Ibid.,
308.

9. God Is the Planetary Mind Field

"To me, the Mind Field resides in a mental energy
field..." Arne A. Wyller, *The Planetary Mind* (Aspen,
Co: MacMurray & Beck, 1996), 231.
"*not* all-powerful... maybe even fallible: *The Planetary
Mind field.*" Ibid., 241.
"The Darwinists and neo-Darwinists... far more time
than the age of the Universe." Ibid., 63.

10. God Is a Playing Intelligence

"in the development of evolution..." Arne A. Wyller, *The
Creating Consciousness: Science as the Language of*

God (Denver, Co: Divina, 1999), 253. This book is an
expanded version of his *The Planetary Mind* book.
"Nature around us bespeaks of its love..." Wyller, *The
Planetary Mind*, 240.
"the number of mystics grows..." Ibid., 242.

11. God Is Creative Intelligence

"the intelligence that conceives..." Chopra, *The Future of
God,* 253.
"That magic word 'evolution'..." Teilhard de Chardin, *The
Heart of Matter* (NY: Harcourt Brace Jovanovich,
1978), 25.

12. God Is the One in Whom We Live

"all things in God and God in all things." Susan
Woodruff, *Meditations with Mechtild of Magdeburg*
(Santa Fe, NM: Bear and Co: 1982), 42.
"ignorant people falsely imagine...completely
enveloping us." Fox, *Passion for Creation*, 73.

13. God Is the All

"God is delighted to watch your soul expand." Fox,
Passion for Creation, 72f.

"all in all....and is one." Ibid., 326, 191.

"that fullness of being in which all things." Hart, *The Experience of God,* 280.

14. God Is the Unity of All Things

"There is only one synonym for God: One." Cited in John C. Merkle, *The Genesis of Faith: The Depth Theology of Abraham Joshua Heschel* (New York: Macmillan, 1985), 80.

"cosmic religion… is oneness of creation, to my sense, is God." Hermanns, *Einstein and the Poet: In Search of the Cosmic Man,* 68f.

"beautiful oneing...and in its creation oned to the Creator." *Doyle, Meditations with Julian of Norwich,* 93.

"in our creation we were knit and oned to God." Ibid., 100.

"I saw a great oneing between Christ and us..." Ibid., 44.

"I know nothing of two worlds" Star, *A Garden Beyond Paradise,* 5.

"we should sink eternally from something to nothing into this One." Fox, *Passion for Creation,* 180.

15. God Is Reality

"is not a being but is at once… as the very act of their existence." Hart, *The Experience of God,* 109.

"unconditioned reality (which, by definition, cannot be temporal or spatial or in any sense finite)…" Ibid., 105f.

"What if God *is* reality?… we are coming to grips with God." Chopra, *The Future of God*, 151f.

16. God Is the Enfolding and Unfolding of Everything That Is

"the absolute, Divine Mind…" James Francis Yockey, *Meditations with Nicolas of Cusa* (Santa Fe, NM: Bear & Co., 1987), 28f.

"universal form of being." Ibid., 131.

17. God Is the Universe

"There is only God." Chopra, *The Future of God,* 253.

"primary sacred reality… sublime dimension of the world about us." Thomas Berry, *The Great Work: Our Way into the Future* (New York: Bell Tower, 1999), 253.

"the universe is the primary revelation of the divine…"
Thomas Berry, "Our Children: Their Future," *The
Little Magazine, Bear & Company*, vol. 1, Number 10,
p. 8.

"Not only are individual creatures images of God." Fox,
Sheer Joy, 66.

"Celebration… exuberant expression of existence itself."
Berry, *The Great Work*, 166.

18. God Is the Self of the Universe

"The self of the Universe." Chopra, *The Future of God*,
253.

"no creature, whether visible or invisible, lacks an
interior life." Matthew Fox, *Hildegard of Bingen: A
Saint For Our Times* (Namaste: Vancouver, Canada,
2012), 56.

19. God Is the Newest and Youngest
Thing in the Universe

"Most youthful." Bose, *The Call of the Vedas*, 211.

"God is novissimus," Fox, *Passion for Creation*, 112.

"In the beginning…" Ibid., 111.

"unborn selves." Ibid., 217.

20. God Is the Ancient One of Ancient Days, the "One Beyond Time."

"God is eternity.....are proper to God." See Ibid., 110-114.
"God is eternal." Hart, *The Experience of God*, 136.

21. God Is Energy

"We know the Holy Spirit....the true door." Thich
   Nhat Hanh, *Going Home: Jesus and Buddha as
   Brothers* (NY: Riverhead, 1999), 101.

24. God Is the Within of Things

"it is proper to God…" Fox, *Passion for Creation*, 163.
"the soul's center is God." Kavanaugh, *The Collected
   Works of St John of the Cross*, 583.
"innermost." Fox, *Passion for Creation*, 65.

25. God Is Consciousness

"God is pure consciousness..." Chopra, *The Future of
   God*, 253.
"Consciousness is creative…." Ibid., 221.

"the fullness of being upon which." Hart, *The Experience of God*, 227.

"the source and ground of the mind's unity..." Ibid., 228.

"infinite consciousness…perfect bliss." Ibid., 237.

"to connect with a mind… the ultimate consciousness that underlies the universe." Rupert Sheldrake, *The Science Delusion: Freeing the Spirit of Enquiry* (London: Coronet, 2012), 237.

"the Great Consciousness of the universe." Ibid., 42-44, 21.

"ought not to exist...we are conscious ourselves." 109, 111.

26. God Is Joy

"God is supremely joyful and…." Fox, *Sheer Joy*, 119.

"Sheer Joy is God's and this demands companionship." Ibid., 100.

"the vibrancy of creation..." Chopra, *The Future of God*, 222.

"God is pure bliss, the source of every human joy." Ibid., 253.

27. God Is Laughter

"When God laughs at the soul..." Fox, *Passion for Creation,* 155.

"God takes sheer delight and laughter over a good deed." Ibid.

"Great Guffaw....Celebrative event." Kristal Parks, *Re-Enchanting the World: A Call to Mystical Activism* (Denver, Colorado: Celebration Press, 2003), 82f.

28. God Is Co-Creator, and the Power of Creation

"over the mind of the artist at work." Fox, *Sheer Joy,* 248.

"I have noticed... with all my heart." Arthur Rubenstein, *My Young Years* (NY: Popular Library, 1973), 488.

"The inescapable fact is that during the 99.9 percent..." Wyller, *The Creating Consciousness,* 254.

29. God Is Greening Power

"The force that through the green fuse..." Cited in John Malcom Brinnin, ed., *A Casebook on Dylan Thomas* (NY: 1965), 3.

"all verdant greening, all creativity…all creation comes from it." Matthew Fox, *Hildegard of Bingen: A Saint for Our Times* (Namaste: Vancouver, Canada, 2012), 12, 92f.

"were meant to green… shriveled barrenness." Ibid., 41.

30. God Is the Artist of Artists

"Every artist loves his work…" Fox, *Sheer Joy,* 64f.

31. God, the Holy Spirit, Is a Rushing River

"rushing river… living waters will flow…" Fox, *A Passion for Creation*, 364, 371, 363.

"the 'Transformer'" Ibid., 369.

32. God Is Flow

"unusually well ordered… purposeful and enjoyable." Mihaly Csikszentmihalyi, *Flow: The Psychology of Optimal Experience* (NY: Harper Perennial, 1990), 41, 40.

"optimal experience… for the sheer sake of doing it." Ibid., 4.

"unfailing flow… a living fountain…" Fox, *Sheer Joy,* 62.

33. God Is Light

"light is a vital ingredient in all atoms..." Wyller, *The Creating Consciousness*, 239.

"God is light;" Fox, *Sheer Joy*, 185f.

"True light that gives light." Fox, *Hildegard of Bingen*, 29f.

"enlightenment... be lamps unto yourself." Cited in Huston Smith, *The Religions of Man* (NY: Harper & Brothers, 1958), 93.

"Krishna is the source of light in all luminous objects." A. C. Bhaktivedanta Swami Prabhupada, *Bhagavad-Gita As It Is* (Los Angeles: The Bhaktivedanta Book Trust, 1986), 661.

"The cosmic waters glow..." Raymundo Panikkar, *The Vedic Experience* (Berkeley, Ca: University of California Press, 1977), 335.

"Radiant in his light... Light that shines within this man." Juan Mascaro, trans., *The Upanishads* (NY: Penguin, 1965), 78.

"How is it possible to tell everyone..." The story is told in Matthew Fox, *A Way To God: Thomas Merton's Creation Spirituality Journey* (Novato, CA: New World Library, 2017), 233.

34. God the Holy Spirit, Is Fire

"Who is the Holy Spirit?" Gabriel Uhlein, *Meditations with Hildegard of Bingen* (Santa Fe, NM: Bear & Co., 1983), 37.

"God glows and burns... this fire is nothing other than the Holy Spirit." Fox, *Passion for Creation*, 289.

"total transformation of the soul in the Beloved... like a blazing fire." Kieran Kavanaugh and Orilio Rodriguez, trans., *The Collected Works of St. John of the Cross* (Washington, D.C.: ICS Publications, 1973), 580f.

35. God Is Compassion

"compassion is the fire that Jesus came to set on Earth." Fox, *Sheer Joy*, 401.

"Humanity is a reminder of God." *Abraham Joshua Heschel Last Words: An Interview by Carl Stern*," Intellectual Digest, June, 1973, p. 78.

"the best name for God is compassion." Fox, *Passion for Creation*, 442.

36. God Is Justice

"God is as it were justice itself." Ibid., 467f.

"compassion means justice." Ibid., 471.

"Compassion is where peace and justice kiss." Ibid., 436.

"For the just person as such to act justly is to live...."
    Ibid., 472.

37. God Is the Great Challenger and the Ground of Conscience

"concern for the unregarded..., a challenging
    transcendence." Cited in Merkle, *The Genesis of
    Faith*, 63.

38. God Is Life

"God is the cause of all life... supereminently alive... and
    ineffable." Fox, *Sheer Joy,* 69.

"most wonderful fact of all... life is alive!" Howard
    Thurman, *Disciplines of the Spirit* (Richmond, IN:
    Friends United Press, 1977), 14.

"radical response to life," See Matthew Fox, *Prayer: A
    Radical Response to Life* (NY: Jeremy Tarcher, 2001).

39. God Is the Beloved

"My Beloved is the mountains..." Kavanaugh, *The Collected Works of St. John of the Cross*, 464-474.

"Creation is allowed in intimate love…" Uhlein, *Meditations with Hildegard of Bingen*, 57.

"The love of God makes…" Doyle, *Meditations with Julian of Norwich*, 113.

"God will appear suddenly and joyfully to all lovers of God." Ibid., 36.

"the lover is not content." Fox, *Sheer Joy*, 78.

"All a Sufi strives for….the goal of all Sufi practice." Star, *A Garden Beyond Paradise*, 3, 79.

"Open your eyes…" Ibid., 99.

40. God Is Beauty

"This then is salvation…" Fox, *Passion For Creation*, 412.

"fountain of total beauty… beauty itself beautifying all things." Fox, *Sheer Joy*, 106, 102.

"supersubstantial beauty…" Ibid., 104.

"is wholly elusive of definition…" Hart, *The Experience of God*, 277.

"recognize creation as the mirror…" Ibid., 284f.

"a supreme and terrible beauty." Yockey, *Meditations with Nicolas of Cusa*, 111.

"God is beautiful and He loves beauty." Star, *A Garden Beyond Paradise*, 158.

41. God Is Truth

"In God lies at once the deepest truth…" Hart, *The Experience of God*, 236.

"They say you bring the word of God…" Star, *A Garden Beyond Paradise*, 57.

"desire alone will rule." Franklin Edgerton, trans., *The Bhagavad Gita*, 16.8 (NY: Harper Torchbooks, 1944), 76.

42. God Is Music

"Who is the Trinity?" Uhlein, *Meditations with Hildegard of Bingen*, 28.

"If there were…" Rupert Sheldrake, *Science and Spiritual Practices* (London: Coronet, 2017), 157.

"are all vibratory… source of life itself." Ibid., 158, 159.

43. God Is an Infinite Voice

"God is an infinite voice… the sound of roaring
thunder." Kavanaugh, *The Collected Works of St. John
of the Cross,* 467, 465.

"gladly doing the best it can to express Divinity." Fox,
Passion for Creation, 59.

"Each of them is endowed with….in testimony to what
God is." Kavanaugh, *The Collected Works of St John of
the Cross,* 472f.

44. God Is Logos or Word

"every creature is a word of God… is full of God and is a
book" Fox, *Passion for Creation,* 58, 79.

"Works of the Lord are the words of the Lord." Fox, *Sheer
Joy,* 60.

"God's Word is in all creation… The word is indivisible
from God." Uhlein, *Meditations with Hildegard of
Bingen,* 49.

45. God Is Wisdom

"the *Logos* of creation in whom all things…" Yockey,
Meditations with Nicolas of Cusa, 112.

"God is the origin of Wisdom." Fox, *Sheer Joy,* 102.

"this is meditation through sucking, not through knowing." Daniel Chanan Matt, trans., *Zohar, the Book of Enlightenment* (NY: Paulist, 1983), 37.

"I, the fiery life of divine wisdom," Uhlein, *Meditations with Hildegard of Bingen*, 30.

46. God Is the Tao

"the Great Mother, Mother of the universe... always present within you." Stephen Mitchell, *Tao Te Ching* (NY: HarperPerennial, 1991), 25, 5.

"flows through all things..." Ibid., 25.

"the universe follows the Tao." Ibid.

"every being in the universe... every being spontaneously honors the Tao." Ibid., 51.

"gives birth to all beings... love of the Tao is in the very nature of things." Ibid.

47. God Is a Circle

"a wheel was shone to me..." Uhlein, *Meditations with Hildegard of Bingen*, 21.

"being is a circle for God." Fox, *Passion for Creation*, 84.

"all things in nature are round…sacred hoop." John G.
   Neihardt, *Black Elk Speaks* (NY: Washington Square
   Press, 1959), 43, 164f.
"Love works in a circle… from their first Source." Fox,
   Sheer Joy, 62, 64.

48. God Is a Source Without a Source

"A source without a source." Ibid., 64.
"the unconditioned source of all things." Hart, *The
   Experience of God*, 134.
"Everything you see has its roots… This is the endless
   Ocean!" *Star, A Garden Beyond Paradise*, 148.

49. God Is Mother

"God feels great delight to be our Mother… God is the
   true Father and Mother of Nature." Doyle,
   Meditations with Julian of Norwich, 94f.
"Pray to the Divine Mother with a longing heart…" Cited
   in Andrew Harvey, ed., *The Essential Mystics: The
   Soul's Journey into Truth* (San Francisco: HarperSan
   Francisco, 1996), 55, 56.

50. God Is Father, Abba

"human cultures the world over." I develop the archetype
of "Father Sky" in considerable depth in chapter one
of Matthew Fox, *The Hidden Spirituality of Men: Ten
Metaphors to Awaken the Sacred Masculine* (Novato,
CA: New World Library, 2008), 3-18.

51. God Is Godhead

"we enter the world of God and creation." See Fox,
Passion for Creation, 75-82.

52. God Is the Final Cause of All Creation

"the final cause of all creation…" Hart, *The Experience
of God*, 286.
"in breakthrough I learn that God and I are one…" Fox,
Passion for Creation, 303.
"our natures have their consummation." Hart, *The
Experience of God*, 287.
"Within its very self nature seeks and strives for God."
Fox, *Passion for Creation*, 63.
"all things desire God…" Fox, *Sheer Joy*, 120.

"the goal of man's life…" Howard Thurman, *Deep River and the Negro Spirituals Speak of Life and Death* (Richmond, IN, Friends United Press, 1996), 27.

53. God Is Our Aspirations

"are the aspiring species." Abrams, *A God That Could Be Real*, 49.
"Aspirations must be real…" Ibid., 50f.
"The emerging God also can be seen…" Ibid., 51.

54. God Is the Beyond

"the individual is not just striving…" E. James Lieberman, *Acts of Will: The Life and Work of Otto Rank* (New York: The Free Press, 1985), 396.
"potential restoration of a union with the Cosmos…" Matthew Fox, *Meister Eckhart: A Mystic-Warrior for Our Times* (Novato, Ca: New World Library, 2014), 144f. I devote a chapter in that book to "Psychotherapy and the 'Unio Mystica': Meister Eckhart Meets Otto Rank," 139-156.

55. God Is "Emmanuel," God-With-Us

"In feminist theology therefore…" Soelle, *Theology for Skeptics,* 49f.

56. God Is the Web of Life

"rather than a climbing of Jacob's ladder." I develop this metaphor at length in Mattthew Fox, *A Spirituality Named Compassion* (Rochester, Vt: Inner Traditions, 1999), Chapter Two, "Sexuality and Compassion: From Climbing Jacob's Ladder to Dancing Sara's Circle," 36-67.

57. God Is the "One Face" that Is Expressed in All the Other Faces in Creation

"In all faces is seen the Face of faces…" Yockey, *Meditations with Nicolas of Cusa,* 139.
"To God belongs the East and the West…" Cited in Star, *A Garden Beyond Paradise,* 157.

58. God Is the Wounds of the Universe and the Wounding in Human Lives as Well

"God's participation in human history..." Abraham
Joshua Heschel, *The Prophets.* (New York: Harper
and Row, 1962), 120

59. God Is the Goddess

"The Goddess in all her manifestations..." Marija
Gimbutas, *The Language of the Goddess* (San
Francisco: HarperSanFrancisco, 1989), 321.

60. God Is Tara

"Our mother: great compassion!" Halle Iglehart Austen,
The Heart of the Goddess (Berkeley: Wingbow Press,
1990), 122.

61. God Is Kuan Yin

"protects women, offers them a religious life...
quenching the flames of distress." Ibid., 44.

62. God Is Oshun

"symbol of the feminine principle." Ibid., 140.

63. God Is Isis

"I am Nature, the universal Mother..." Ibid., 48.

"As mother and earth woman…" Cited in Eloise
    McKinney-Johnson, "Egypt's Isis: The Original black
    Madonna," *Journal of African Civilizations*, vol 6,
    n.1, April, 1984, 68.

64. God Is the Black Madonna

"life, life with all its teeming diversity…" China Galland,
    Longing for Darkness: Tara and the Black Madonna
    (NY: Viking, 1990), 156f.

"the cosmos, people of color, and much more." I have
    elaborated on this archetype of the Black Madonna
    and propose a "sacred marriage" of her and the
    Green Man in Fox, *The Hidden Spirituality of Men*,
    231-244.

65. God Is Kali

"the collective dark night that our globe finds itself in
    today." See Andrew Harvey and Carolyn Baker,
    Savage Grace (Bloomington, IN: iUniverse
    Publishers, 2017).

66. God Is Mary

"ground of all being… in you, mild virgin, is the
    fullness of all joy." Uhlein, *Meditations with
    Hildegard of Bingen*, 115f.
"luminous mother, holy, healing art… delicious ecstasy
    that is forever yours." Ibid, 117f.
"Mother of all joy… buds forth into light." Ibid., 118f.
"whatever was irregular, exceptional, outlawed…" R. P.
    Blackmur, *Henry Adams* (New York: Harcourt,
    Brace, Jovanovich, 1980), 204.
"a Unity that brought… to stunt any of them." Ibid.,
    204, 206.
"above law… the idea of sorrowful contemplation."
    Ibid., 203.

67. God Is Our Lady of Guadalupe

"a warrior goddess who blessed… on behalf of women's rights." Ann Castillo, ed., *Goddess of the Americas: Writings on the Virgin of Guadalupe* (New York: Riverhead Books, 1996), 180.

69. God Is Gaia

"The earth is at the same time mother…" Uhlein, *Meditations with Hildegard of Bingen,* 58.

70. God Is Chaos

"considered the source of evil." See Carol Christ, *Rebirth of the Goddess* (New York: Addison-Wesley, 1997), 66.
"she has returned as a goddess." See Ralph Abraham, *Chaos, Gaia, Eros: A Chaos Pioneer Uncovers the three Great Stories of History* (San Francisco: HarperSanFrancisco, 1994).

71. God Is the Trinity

"sexuality, sensuality and creativity." Austen, *The Heart of the Goddess,* xix.

"God is the one act… being, consciousness, and bliss."
Hart, *The Experience of God*, 249, 132.

"In the Name of the Bee…" Thomas H. Johnson, ed.,
The Complete Poems of Emily Dickinson (New York:
Basic Books, 1961) #18.

"her medicine womanhood." See Steven Herrmann,
*Emily Dickinson: A Medicine Woman for Our Time*s
(Sheridan, Wy: Fisher King Press, 2018).

72. God Is the Holy One

"the word holiness… the mystery and majesty of the
divine." Heschel, *The Sabbath*, 9.

"part of holiness." I have reproduced this marvelous
poem fittingly in a chapter on "Living Words and
the Cosmic Christ: Hildegard meets Mary Oliver" in
Fox, *Hildegard of Bingen*, 18-22.

73. God Is the Cosmic Christ

"the Blinding One speaks to us gently…" Fox, *A Way to
God*, 232.

"Cosmic Christ is Cosmic Wisdom." I have treated
the theme of the Cosmic Christ in Matthew Fox,
The Coming of the Cosmic Christ (San Francisco:

HarperSanFrancisco, 1988); and again with Bishop Marc Andrus and two artists in Stations of the Cosmic Christ (San Francisco, CA: Tayen Lane Publishing, 2016).

74. God Is the Ultimate "I Am"

"only God is the necessary one." Hart, *The Experience of God*, 109.

75. God Is a Lion and Destroyer of Darkness and Evil

"Destroyer of Darkness and Evil." Bose, *The Call of the Vedas*, 211.

"it may be the greatest evolutionary gamble... extinguish the human element of evil." Wyller, *The Planetary Mind*, 239.

"the imperfect coupling between... the attributes of the Mind Field." Ibid., 238f

76. God Is the True Rest

"our true resting place." Doyle, *Meditations with Julian of Norwich*, 26.

"God enjoys the divine nature which is repose." Fox,
    Passion for Creation, 384.
"Nothing resembles God so much as repose." Ibid., 385.

77. God Is a Great Bird

"moving force of Wisdom." Fox, *Hildegard of Bingen*, 86.
"the transcendent nature of God, the One who can fly
    anywhere." Star, *A Garden Beyond Paradise*, 156.
"You are the great bird of Mount Sinai…" Ibid., 96.

78. God Is the Wilderness and Destroyer

"There is no room for two in the desert…" Fox, *Passion
    for Creation*, p. 393.
"God leads this spirit into the desert…" Ibid., 361.
"every serious religious tradition admits of this 'terrible'
    aspect of the Godhead." Bede Griffiths, *Return to the
    Center,* (Springfield, IL: Templegate Publishers,
    1976), 89.

79. God Is the Transcendent Care of All Creatures

"the transcendent care for being." Abraham J. Heschel,
    Who Is Man? (Stanford, CA: Stanford University
    Press, 1965), 91.

"Council of All Beings." See John Seed, Joanna Macy, et al, *Thinking Like A Mountain: Towards a Council of All Beings* (Gabriola Island, BC, Canada, 1988).

80. God Is the Kingdom of God

"The promise of God's kingdom is that people…" Bruce Chilton, *The Way of Jesus: To Repair and Renew the World* (Nashville, TN: Abingdon Press, 2010), 73f. See also Fox, *Meister Eckhart*, 107-109.

"we have a right to translate it as creation." A private conversation.

Part II: Names for the God Without a Name

"the Divine One is none of these beings…" Fox, *Sheer Joy*, 183.

"No one can really say what God is." Fox, *Passion for Creation*, 175.

"Language cannot do everything…" Adrienne Rich, *The Dream of a Common Language* (NY: Norton, 1978), 19.

81. God Is the Uncreated One

"God is uncreated." Chopra, *The Future of God*, 253.

"Let's assume that God is infinite." Chopra, *God: A Story of Revelation*, 2.

82. God Is Superessential Darkness

"superessential darkness… darkness beyond light." Rolt, *Dionysius the Areopagite*, 196, 194.

"the final end is the mystery of the darkness of the eternal Godhead." Fox, *Passion for Creation*, 175.

83. God Is the Great Mystery

"The mystery of the darkness…" Ibid.

"reflect upon the mystery that manifests… when we surrender ourselves to it." Hart, *The Experience of God*, 329, 331.

84. God Is the Ineffable One

"Ineffable One… a truly hidden God." Fox, *Passion for Creation*, 175.

"we know the Holy Spirit as energy…" Thich Naht Hanh, *Going Home*, 101.

85. God Is the Unknown One

"The cause at which we wonder is hidden from us..."
Fox, *Sheer Joy*, 195.

"Reason can never comprehend God..." Fox, *Passion for Creation*, 442.

"greatest achievement [is] to realize that God..." Fox, *Sheer Joy*, 196.

"whatever one says what God is, God is not..." Fox, *Passion for Creation*, 175.

"befriend the unknown... the certainty of the known for the unknown." Estelle Frankel, *The Wisdom of Not Knowing: Discovering a Life of Wonder by Embracing Uncertainty* (Boulder, Colorado: Shambhala, 2017), xi, 1.

"being receptive to the unknown..." Ibid., 1f.

"always involves a synergy of knowing and not knowing..." Ibid., 3.

86. God Is Nothingness

"God is said to be non-being..." Fox, *Sheer Joy*, 207.

"God is a being beyond being... a nameless nothingness." Fox, *Passion for Creation*, 178f.

"God is nothing..." Ibid., 194.

"We cannot name Brahman…" Bede Griffiths, *The Cosmic Revelation: The Hindu Way to God* (Springfield, IL: Templegate Publishers, 1983), 54.

"*Ayin*, Nothingness, is more existent than all the being of the world…" Daniel C. Matt, *The Essential Kabbalah* (San Francisco: HarperSanFrancisco, 1996), 66f.

"Relation accordingly is present…" Fox, *Passion for Creation*, 198.

87. God Is the Annihilation of Thought

"that which thought cannot comprehend." Matt, *Zohar*, 176.

"All is one in the… it is called Nothingness, Ayin." Matt, *The Essential Kabbalah*, 66f.

"the one who never speaks about God." Thich Naht Hahn, *Going Home*, 8.

"The most beautiful thing which a person…" Fox, *Passion for Creation*, 182.

88. God Is the Form Without Form

"seamless, unnamable, it returns…" Mitchell, *Tao Te Ching*, 14.

"God is a not God….who is separate from all twoness."
Fox, *Passion for Creation*, 180.

89. God Is Silence

"Nothing in all creation is so like God as silence…
which is the source of all things." Fox, *Meister
Eckhart: A Mystic-Warrior for Our Times*. 39.
"The Word lies hidden in the soul…" Ibid., 40.
"Secretly we spoke…" Star, *A Garden Beyond Paradise*, 35.
"Silence means no repetitions…" Nana Veary, *Change
We Must: My Spiritual Journey* (Honolulu, HI:
Institute of Zen Studies, 1989), 103f.
"Evidently, our brains are hardwired…" Frankel, *The
Wisdom of Not Knowing*, 3f.

Appendix

"Even the very ones who were experienced… insofar as
God surpasses all things." Fox, *Sheer Joy*, 182f.

Acknowledgements

A topic as foundational as "Names of God" has many parents of course and so I must give thanks to the many mystics East and West whom I call on in this book with a special shout out to the thinkers of old such as Dennis the Areapogyte and his classic work *On the Divine Names* and of course St Thomas Aquinas' Commentary on the same. Gratitude to Meister Eckhart confessing that "I pray God to rid me of God" and to Hildegard of Bingen, Rumi, Deepak Chopra and David Hart. As we evolve, personally and collectively, our understandings of God evolve also (or at least ought to). There is the teaching and practice of the "99 Most Beautiful Names of God" that has been gifted to us from the Sufi mystical tradition of Islam and to which I am gratefully indebted.

Thank you also to the scientists I invoke including Erich Jantsch, Albert Einstein, Arne Wyller (who was humble enough to attend a book reading I did years ago in Santa Fe and kind enough to introduce himself and his work to me afterwards), Rupert Sheldrake (who introduced me to Hart's important work as well as continues his many major contributions to spirituality and science), Nancy Abrams, Thomas Berry, Brian Swimme and more.

In the concrete I want to thank Theodore Richards for his fine editing and suggestions for improving this book along the way including refining the title to what it is today. And Leslie Browning for her leadership with her edgy publishing venture and her sensitivity and promptness and encouragement throughout this process.

Also a shout out to Ullrrich Javier Lemus for his wonderful artistry that graces the book's cover called "The Cosmic Black Madonna." To Dennis Edwards for his steadfast and long-term commitment to the Creation Spirituality tasks that arise in his capacity as my assistance and to Phila Hoopes for her work on the web page and twitter and to Mary Plaster for her assistance with the Facebook page. To Aaron Stern and the Academy for the Love of Learning for their encouragement and support over a number of years. And to Ron Tuazon and Mara too for the inspiring personal support they lend me on a daily basis.

About the Author

MATTHEW FOX, who holds a doctorate in the history and theology of spiritualities from the Institut catholique de Paris, is author of 35 books on spirituality and culture that have been translated into 69 languages and received many awards. A partial list of these books is offered at the front of this book. Since learning of the Creation Spirituality tradition from his mentor, Pere M. D. Chenu, Fox has dedicated his life to recovering that lineage and bringing it alive. Accordingly he founded graduate programs in Culture and Creation Spirituality at colleges in Chicago and then Oakland and developed a cutting edge educational pedagogy that includes artists, scientists, mystics of all traditions and activists to teach spirituality that includes intellect and intuition, body, heart and mind.

Since Creation Spirituality is both a mystical and a prophetic tradition, Fox's support of women and gay rights, of the environment and social, racial and gender justice and of liberation theology disturbed naysayers in the Vatican which silenced him for a year and then pressured the Dominican Order to dismiss him after 34 years.

Subsequently he founded the University of Creation Spirituality (UCS) in Oakland California and became an Episcopal priest to work with young people to create a post-modern worship form called *the Cosmic Mass* which incorporates dance, dj, vj, rap and other post-modern art forms. Most recently he has launched, along with a 28 year old and a 33 year old leader, an *Order of the Sacred Earth* which is a spiritual (not religious) order open to people of all traditions and none who feel called to focus their commitment to save the earth and the people and critters on it with a common vow to be "the best lover and the best defender of Earth that I can be." A new school called the *Fox Institute for Creation Spirituality* has recently been launched in Boulder, Colorado by some of the graduates of UCS. He is a visiting scholar with the Academy for the Love of Learning in Santa Fe, New Mexico founded by Leonard Bernstein and Aaron Stern.

He lives in the Bay Area in northern California. Among the awards granted him have been the Gandhi-King-Ikeda Peace Award from Morehouse College, the Humanities Award of the Sufi International Association of Sufism, the Tikkun Ethics Award, and the Courage of Conscience Award from the Peace Abbey of Sherborn, Massachusetts. Other recipients of this award include the Dalai Lama, Mother Teresa, Rosa Parks, Ernesto Cardinale and Maya Angelou.

www.matthewfox.org

**HOMEBOUND
PUBLICATIONS**

Ensuring that the mainstream isn't the only stream.

At Homebound Publications, we publish books written by independent voices for independent minds. Our books focus on a return to simplicity and balance, connection to the earth and each other, and the search for meaning and authenticity. Founded in 2011, Homebound Publications is one of the rising independent publishers in the country. Collectively through our imprints, we publish between fifteen to twenty offerings each year. Our authors have received dozens of awards, including: *Foreword Reviews'* Book of the Year, Nautilus Book Award, Benjamin Franklin Book Awards, and Saltire Literary Awards. Highly-respected among bookstores, readers and authors alike, Homebound Publications has a proven devotion to quality, originality and integrity.

We are a small press with big ideas. As an independent publisher we strive to ensure that the mainstream is not the only stream. It is our intention at Homebound Publications to preserve contemplative storytelling. We publish full-length introspective works of creative non-fiction as well as essay collections, travel writing, poetry, and novels. In all our titles, our intention is to introduce new perspectives that will directly aid humankind in the trials we face at present as a global village.

WWW.HOMEBOUNDPUBLICATIONS.COM

Printed in the USA
CPSIA information can be obtained
at www.ICGtesting.com
JSHW022321140824
68134JS00019B/1228

9 781947 003941